Congrats to Igor from S‹

Alan Alda:
"Can't wait to try the recipes. There are several people I'm trying to kill."

Wayne Rogers:
"I thought Igor ate raw meat! What a surprise! He can cook!"

Mike Farrell:
"I wouldn't touch this stuff with a pitchfork!"

David Ogden Stiers:
"What a great potential diet plan—an entire cookbook filled with inedible results."

Jamie Farr:
"If an Army travels on its stomach—this is the cook and book we couldn't stomach!"

Harry Morgan:
"The Lost Recipes of Private Igor? There seems to be a misconception here—those recipes weren't lost! We did our best to hide them. Frankly, we thought nobody would give a damn. It's hard to accept that we might have been wrong—so we won't."

Larry Linville:
"I love Igor's serving style—glop glop, plop plop, and 'move along!'"

Gary Burghoff:
"Igor taught me why they call it a mess."

Loretta Swit:
"A cookbook from Igor, what a delightful idea—who better to feed a nation. On the other hand, I think it's dangerous. I think it's just the thing that could start another war!"

Bill Christopher:
"What? A cookbook from Igor?! What will be next, a restaurant? I sense this could easily get out of hand."

Burt Metcalfe (M*A*S*H Executive Producer):
"Igor's food brings a whole new meaning to the term 'take out.'"

Walter Dishell (M*A*S*H Medical Advisor):
"A cookbook from Igor? Take two antacids and call me in the morning!"

Secrets of
The
M*A*S*H
Mess

Secrets of
The
M*A*S*H
Mess

THE LOST RECIPES OF
PRIVATE IGOR

JEFF MAXWELL

CUMBERLAND HOUSE

NASHVILLE, TENNESSEE

*I dedicate this book
to my beautiful wife, Sherie.*

Published by Cumberland House Publishing, Inc.
431 Harding Industrial Park Drive, Nashville, Tennessee 37211

Design by Bruce Gore, Gore Studio Inc., Nashville, Tennessee.

Distributed to the trade by Andrews and McMeel
4520 Main Street, Kansas City, Missouri 64111-7701

Library of Congress Cataloging-in-Publication Data

Maxwell, Jeff
Secrets of the M*A*S*H mess : the lost recipes of Private Igor / Jeff Maxwell
p.   cm.
Includes index.
ISBN 1-888952-41-5 (paperback : alk. paper)
1. Cookery.   2. MASH (Television program)   I. Title.
TX741.M3785 1997
641.5—dc21   97-27811
                                                   CIP

Printed in the United States of America
1 2 3 4 5 6 7 — 01 00 99 98 97

• CONTENTS •

SPECIAL ACKNOWLEDGMENTS

To Larry Gelbart and Gene Reynolds go my heartfelt, everlasting appreciation for responding to me with swift, familial goodness when I needed you. Thank you for letting me play a small part in your inspiring television achievement.

To Henry Bloomstein, whose outstanding contribution to this material helped prevent me from sounding like a chimp. Thank you for your unrelenting belief in this project, your perspicacious modifiers, and our triple decade friendship.

Mr. Ron Pitkin, President of Cumberland House Publishing, thank you for all the great phone conversations, and your wonderful decision to publish this book.

Mrs. Julie Pitkin, thank you for your guidance and charming patience.

A special thank you to Frankie Carlisle, owner of Frankie's, a very popular restaurant in Tarzana, California, who worked so diligently with me to bring out all the zesty flavors found in Igor's original creations. His artful contributions to the recipes are an invaluable part of this book. A native of Beaumont, Texas, Frankie learned his way around a kitchen from his Italian and Cajun neighbors. If you're ever in Tarzana, please stop in and say hello to Frankie—tell him Igor sent you.

And...

My brother, "bubba Ron," for making me laugh so hard about the mule. My mother and father for letting me act goofy whenever I wanted. Len Smith Jr. for shoving my face in front of the camera. Roy Goldman and Dennis Troy for their nine years of humor and stimulating political diversity. William F. Goergens, and Bill Garrett, my friend and partner who helped me develop whatever comedy ability I have. Bruce Maidy for getting me that first job. Royce Bemis for finding the right path. Lori Winchester for her celestial friendship. Jerry Lewis for teaching me comedic timing while I was trying to be him. And, in no particular order: Mark Hobson, Diane Burroughs, Craig and Patti Spencer, Katherine Drago, Cory Eglash, Jacqueline Green, Gina Goldman, Rick Rosen, Margaret Anderson, Richard Salvetore, Michael Hirsh, Laurens Schwartz, George Bellias and Jade Productions, and all the good folks at Twentieth Century Fox: Mr. Rupert Murdoch, Jennifer Sebree, Patrick Miller, Debbie Olshan, Dionne Dominique Ferguson.

I would also like to thank the following people who were generous enough to share some delicious secrets with me: Ronnie Knott, Ann Gravelle, Connie Miyajima, Laurin Rinder, Josephine Knott, Norma Weiss, Rick Waln, Diane Burroughs, Bernie Knott, Richard Salvetore, Minsoo Moutes-Lee, Mark Hobson, Lori Winchester, Kyle Cole, Kaye Crawford, Faye and Jerry Robinson, Donna Strandt, Shelby Yates, Morgan Gallagher, Jerry Clifford, Arlene Barnett, Marla Berk, Janet Nassiri.

• FOREWORD •

BY ALAN ALDA

I got a letter in the mail from a certain Jeff Maxwell who claimed to have written a cookbook based on what was served by Igor in the MASH mess tent. This is an extremely humorous idea. No food of that kind has ever been the subject of a book, except one written in the 1500s by Lucretia Borgia.

I ate Igor's ragout for eleven years. Actually, I mostly just smelled it, but molecules of it can get into your bloodstream through your nose and if anyone actually cooks from this book, they better wear a surgical mask. It's been documented that the Korean war would have ended six months earlier if they had dropped Igor's food on the enemy instead of using bombs.

This unusual book has many uses. Almost any recipe can be used as an effective substitute for mace. Carry a piece of Igor's liver in your handbag and you'll never fear walking down a dark street again. I also heartily recommend this book to anyone suffering from an overpopulation of deer. Just leave one of these dishes next to your azaleas and you will never see another deer as long as you live.

I certainly wish Jeff the best with this project and I hope Igor gets so rich from his share of the profits that he doesn't have to eat any of his own cooking ever again.

—Benjamin Franklin Pierce, Capt. U.S. Army, Ret.
(As told to Alan Alda)

• ANOTHER FOREWORD •
BY LARRY GELBART

Perhaps the oldest army joke in the world has one soldier saying to another: "I saved my regiment. I shot the cook." With the substitution of a spear for a bullet, the joke probably goes back to days of the Roman Legions, for while it is true that an army travels on its stomach, the poor quality of the chow it lives on makes a good deal of that travel trips to the latrine.

There is, of course, no reason for life to imitate art when it comes to indigestion, heartburn and worse. The food served in the *M*A*S*H* mess tent, prepared by the commissary at Twentieth Century Fox was a whole lot more palatable than the real thing.

Enter the fertile brain and creative bent of Jeff Maxwell, the much beloved and frequently berated Igor of 4077th fame.

This book of "lost" recipes is the result of an imagination and an antic spirit that Jeff brought to the series on a daily, weekly, and yearly basis. He was a valued member of the cast and a joy to work with, transforming Igor into a far more interesting character in the flesh than he ever was in the pages of the script.

I commend you on this book, Jeff. I couldn't put it down. I'll leave that to the critics.

If you want to join me for breakfast we can have a stack of pancreas.
—HAWKEYE

• PREFACE •
BY GENE REYNOLDS

When I first heard there was to be a book of recipes by Private Igor I assumed it was some kind of cruel joke. I chuckled and then experienced severe heartburn. The idea of this outrageous man doing further damage to American stomachs unnerved me. The men and women of *M*A*S*H* often muttered bitterly that war was hell, anguish inspired partly by the trials of combat and largely by the trauma of Igor's mess tent meals.

Some feel that Igor did not intend to be destructive; that he did not purposely try to poison an entire MASH unit. However, some men cannot be trusted with guns and some should not be handed a spatula. Weapons in the wrong hands can be a terrible thing. Fortunately, the lives of many were saved because their stomachs were fortified with alcohol.

One mystery of the war remains. An inexplicable reversal of fortune for the United Nations troops occurred just as the north was about to overrun the south. The enemy suddenly stopped, staggered back, and retreated. History credits the tactics of General Douglas MacArthur with his amphibious operation that outflanked the northern invaders. Recent evidence indicates there was a dramatic collapse of the enemy shortly after their occupation of a MASH unit's canteen. Something traumatized the invaders and sent them stumbling, reeling off to the north.

Is it possible the Congressional Medal of Honor really belongs to a misfit chef of middle European origin? Will MacArthur's family accept the transfer of honors to this culinary cuckoo? For the morale of America, we may have to perpetuate another cover-up. In this case, can the world blame us?

Before reading this book, drink hot tea laced with Pepto Bismol. Follow the buddy system and have a friend at your side at all times. Do not leave this book within reach of small children.

Gene Reynolds, Larry Gelbart and director, Hy Averback show Igor how to work a projector.

• INTRODUCTION •

BY JEFF MAXWELL

Every day, long before reveille, one lone, dedicated, lackluster private, known only as Igor, made his way through the cold early-morning air, to the mess tent of the 4077. It was there that he literally served his country by slopping meal after meal onto a seemingly endless parade of metal trays. Braced for imminent assault, poor Igor daily took all the heat for the prevailing "minus four star" cuisine he was forced to dish out. Never flinching or deserting his post, he persevered behind his steam table, heroically enduring the verbal grenades of the outraged *M*A*S*H* company:

"You've creamed weenies?"

And...

"I've eaten a river of liver and an ocean of fish. I want something else!"
Since his horrendous culinary tour of duty, Igor has virtually dropped out of sight. He has never been seen on any of the *M*A*S*H* TV reunions, nor has he been in touch with his family for years. It's more than likely that the humiliation he suffered as a military chef caused him to change his identity and take up a new life somewhere.

Reports of his current whereabouts are random, sketchy and difficult to confirm. Some leads indicate that he's been active on the swap-meet circuit, trading heavily in antique kitchen utensils. Other tips suggest that he made big bucks as a hog farmer, turned into an eccentric recluse, and now lives somewhere in Kansas close to a meat packing plant. According to one informant, he went back to school and became a licensed hypnotherapist, which led to a lucrative Beverly Hills practice. Unfortunately, he was hit with a whopping malpractice suit by a famous chain-smoking pop singer. As the story goes, Igor stowed away on a plane to Bucharest, and hasn't been seen since.

Recently, I made a startling discovery which signals good news for this much-maligned soldier's legion of fans. While rummaging through my Uncle Hank's attic for garage sale treasures, I came across a stack of musty *Life* magazines from the 1950's. Slipped in between the various issues were old letters written by my cousin, Igor, to his mother. With warmth, humor, and surprising gastronomic savvy, the *M*A*S*H* 4077's "kitchen ghoul" reveals himself to be an imaginative, uncommonly-gifted chef.

Shackled by having to cook and serve basic Army swill, Igor innocently concocted more "creative" alternatives—the very recipes that made their way into these letters. My friend, restaurant owner Frankie Carlisle, graciously volunteered to help me translate Igor's instinctive—and surprisingly inventive—ideas into the delicious recipes contained herein. Publishing them, I believe, will help fully restore my beleaguered cousin's culinary reputation. I further trust that good reviews and enthusiastic public support will only encourage him to come forward and enjoy the accolades he has so long deserved.

While some may speculate about the importance of one M*A*S*H character over another, it cannot be denied that surviving the awesome responsibility of "nourishing" every single member of the camp—three times a day—makes Igor an important, if not pivotal, member of the entire ensemble.

Make no mistake about it: This is a cookbook offering an eclectic combination of delicious meals, carefully planned to satisfy a variety of tastes. Followed to the letter, I guarantee that every recipe created by Igor will satisfy the heartiest of appetites.

It is with a great pride, then, that I present to the 4077's loyal fans—readers and eaters alike—*Secrets of The M*A*S*H Mess: The Lost Recipes of Private Igor.*

Bon Appetit!

IGOR: Okay, okay, excuse me for living.
CHARLES: There is no excuse for your living.

Dear *M*A*S*H* Fans,

    I made every effort to maintain the integrity of Igor's recipes as discovered by Jeff Maxwell. His thoroughly modern concepts and exciting combination of spices remain exactly as they were written. Only measurement and amount descriptions such as "A halfa handfula salt" and "A medium lumpa meat" were areas that I felt needed some definition and refinement.

    As a fellow chef, it was a real pleasure to have contributed to this remarkable discovery. After all, when one thinks of Private Igor, quality and taste do not instantly leap to mind—until now.

—Frankie Carlisle

You think show business is easy?

Dear Ma,

Hello from Korea. I'm in the middle of nowhere tucked in between some mountains at the MASH 4077th. The letters stand for Mobil Army Surgical Hospital. It's like Saint Luke at home except all the buildings are just tents so they can be folded up and moved in a couple of hours. It's just like a little city here. There's a hospital, a garage, a bar, an airport, police, and a Mayor (we call him Colonel). Oh yeah, and a restaurant, except the Army calls it a Mess Tent, and boy, do I know why! Ha, ha.

Love, Igor

Dear Ma,

The day I got here, this doctor, Lieutenant Burns, made me take a test to find out if I'm good at anything. It said I should be fixing trucks. Wow. YOU could've told'em that nobody keeps the Pontiac running like Igor. Anyway, it looks like I get to be in the Motor Pool! Don't worry about me not knowing how to swim, it's not that kind of pool—ha, ha. MY job'll be to keep our jeeps and ambulances running good in case we ever have to bug outta here. Well, I gotta go. We get to watch a movie tonight and I have to run the projector. (I think the movie is "Prisoner of Zenda" with Tyrone Power.)

Hope the Pontiac is still purring like Candy the cat, ha, ha. Love to you and Pop.

Love, Igor

Dear Ma,

Sorry to write with bad news, but guess what? I still can't believe it. Instead of letting me work at something I'm good at, they're gonna make me do a job I don't know anything about! Radar, the Company Clerk here, told me that he thinks the Army does that on purpose. Do you think so? Anyway, some guy in the Mess tent got this disease that makes you so tired you can't help from passing out. The other day he fell asleep in the soup pot and got shipped home. (Not in the pot!) They told me, if I can fry an egg, I hafta take his place. Hope you're still proud of me. Oh yeah, don't say anything to Janine about the Mess thing. I haven't told her yet. I'm gonna miss working on the trucks.

Love, Igor

Dear Ma,

I don't mean to gripe but this cooking thing is really hard! It's gonna make me nuts. I get up before everybody else to fix up the Mess Tent and help cook. Then I have to stand behind this long table with hot steam shooting out of it and serve breakfast to every single person who comes in. That's EVERYBODY IN THE CAMP! Ma, I don't mean to gripe, but nobody can stand the food and they really let me know about it. Anyway, as soon as breakfast is over, I gotta start making lunch and then dinner. I usually get through cleaning up about nine-thirty and have just enough energy left to get a beer, I mean a coke, and then fall into my bunk. Then, I gotta get up and start it all over again. The worst part of the whole thing is that I gotta wear an apron and a real goofy look-ing white hat.

                    Love, Igor.
PS Please don't tell anybody about me wear-ing the apron thing, especially Cousin Candace!

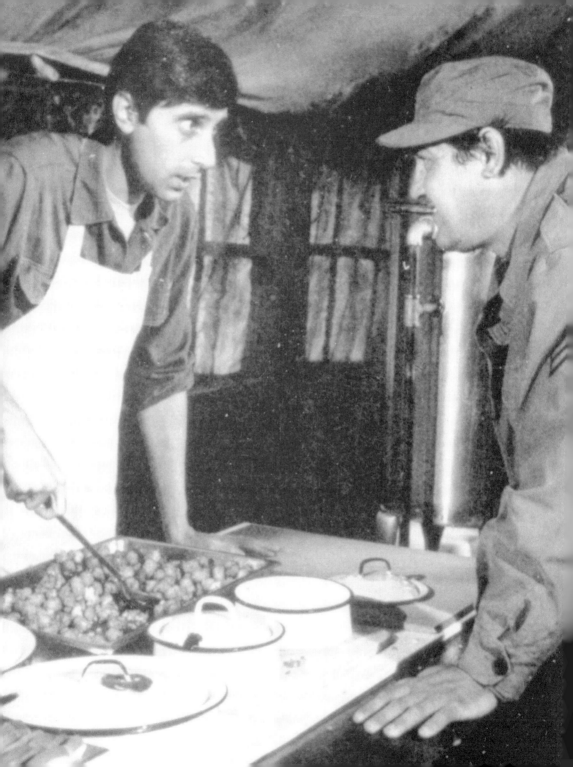

• BREAKFAST •

EGGS OVER & OVER

Incoming Eggs

Serves 4

8	eggs
2	tablespoons milk
1½	teaspoons unsalted butter or margarine
1	4-ounce can sliced mushrooms, drained
2	plum tomatoes, seeded and chopped
1	green bell pepper, seeded and chopped
1	yellow onion, chopped
1	cup chopped cooked ham or sausage
4	slices American, Cheddar, or Swiss cheese

1. In a large bowl beat the eggs. Add the milk and beat again. In a large skillet with a lid melt the butter until bubbly. Pour the eggs into the skillet and cook, uncovered, until they start to set.

2. Stir in all the vegetables and meat. Continue to stir as if making scrambled eggs. Spread the mixture into an even layer around the pan. Turn the heat down very low. Place the cheese slices on top of the eggs then cover for about 5 minutes, letting the cheese melt into the eggs.

3. Divide the omelet and transfer to individual plates. Serve with toast.

IV Eggs and Sausage

Serves 2

1	tablespoon olive oil
⅓	yellow onion, finely chopped
1	jalapeño pepper, seeded and minced
1	teaspoon fresh garlic, chopped
6	eggs, beaten
14	ounces Andouille sausage, cooked and diced (bake at 400° for 10 minutes)

1. Preheat the broiler.

2. In a large nonstick skillet or sauté pan heat the olive oil over medium heat. Add the onion, jalapeño pepper, and garlic and sauté for 3 minutes.

3. Add the eggs and sausage and cook until lightly browned on the bottom. Place under the broiler until the top of the omelet turns golden brown.

4. Divide the omelet and transfer to individual plates. Serve.

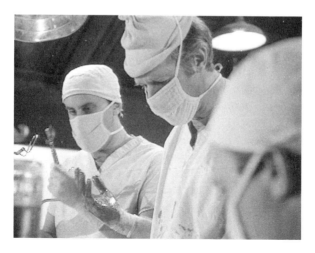

Look Ma, it's "Doctor" Igor operatin' with a can opener. Ha ha.

Dear Ma,

This may sound like a funny question, but did you and Pop make any money with the machine shop you invested in? The reason I ask, there's a doctor here named Trapper who the nurses get all stupid over. They say he looks like a movie actor. I look like a movie actor too, but I guess it's not one the nurses like. Ha ha. Anyway, one day I find him layin' flat on a mess table 'cause he hurt his back playin' catch with Lt. Dish, and for no reason at all, I start talkin' to him about money. Ma, this guy is a good doctor but he knows a lot about investin' and stuff. He told me that back in the world, people even gave him their money to invest for them. If you want to send me a bunch, I'll give it to him, I promise!

Love, Igor

P.S. I'm sending some more ideas you and Pop can make for breakfast. Don't tell anybody, but it's kinda fun experimentin' with different things than the Army lets us make. If you like my recipes, write to Colonel Potter and tell him. Maybe he'll let me cook the way I want to too! Ha ha.

BREAKFAST

Klinger's Section 8 Omelet

Serves 2

1	tablespoon unsalted butter
1	cup chopped fresh spinach
½	cup diced salami
1	cup sliced fresh mushrooms
4	eggs, beaten
1	dash jalapeño Tabasco sauce
	Salt and pepper to taste

1. Preheat the broiler.
2. In a medium sauté pan melt the butter over medium-high heat. Add the spinach and salami and cook for 1 minute. Add the mushrooms, eggs, Tabasco, salt, and pepper and cook until lightly browned on the bottom. Place under the broiler until the top of the omelet turns golden brown.
3. Divide the omelet and transfer to individual plates. Serve.

*Not all of us have nice
gloves like Klinger.*

Mrs. O'Reilly's Farmhouse Omelet

Serves 3 to 4

1	tablespoon unsalted butter
1	yellow onion, chopped
1	potato, diced
4	slices bacon, chopped
½	cup chopped mushrooms
3	large eggs
2	tablespoons milk
¼	teaspoon dried herbs
	Salt and pepper to taste
1	cup grated Cheddar cheese

1. Preheat the broiler.

2. In a medium skillet melt the butter over medium heat. Add the onion, potato, and bacon and simmer until soft. Add the mushrooms, then increase the heat and cook until the vegetables begin to brown.

3. In a medium bowl beat the eggs, milk, and herbs together, and season with salt and pepper. Pour over the bacon and vegetables, tilting the skillet to spread evenly. Cook over medium heat until the omelet starts to set.

4. Sprinkle the omelet with cheese and place under the broiler, keeping the door ajar. Cook until the cheese is bubbly and golden brown.

5. Divide the omelet and transfer to individual plates. Serve.

Radar and me gettin' caught by Major Houlihan.

"This is the Army.
Nobody can do
the best he can."
—COLONEL BLAKE

• 7 •

BREAKFAST

Pierce's Poached Eggs

with Shrimp and Crawfish

Serves 4

2	tablespoons unsalted butter
2	cloves fresh garlic, finely minced
2	tablespoons fresh lemon juice
⅓	cup dry white wine
¼	pound (25 to 30) small shrimp, shelled and deveined
1	6-ounce can Aunt Pennies' Hollandaise sauce
¼	pound cooked crawfish (or fresh crab meat or more shrimp)
1	dash Tabasco sauce
1	dash Worcestershire sauce
4	large eggs
4	sourdough English muffin halves
	Paprika

1. In a medium saucepan melt the butter over medium-high heat. Add the garlic, lemon juice, and wine, and bring to a boil. Add the shrimp, reduce the heat slightly, and sauté for 2 minutes. Transfer the shrimp immediately to a medium mixing bowl and cover to keep warm.

2. In a small saucepan combine the Hollandaise sauce, crawfish, Tabasco, and Worcestershire sauce and warm slowly over very low heat, stirring occasionally.

3. In a large saucepan bring 1½ inches of water to a boil. Reduce the heat. Break an egg into a cup then slide the egg carefully into the water. Repeat with each egg. Toast the English muffins while the eggs simmer for 3 to 5 minutes or until the whites are firm and the yolks are still soft.

4. Place the muffins on individual plates. Gently remove the eggs from the water with a slotted spoon, drain well, and place one on each muffin. Pour equal portions of the crawfish mixture over each egg, then top with the shrimp. Lightly sprinkle each with paprika. Serve.

BREAKFAST

Sidney Freedman's
Nervous Breakdown Breakfast

Scrambled Eggs and Lox on English Muffins

Serves 2

6	large eggs
6	tablespoons half and half
	Freshly ground pepper to taste
¼	cup unsalted butter
4	ounces lox or smoked salmon, chopped
2	English muffins, halved and toasted

1. In a medium bowl whisk the eggs and half and half. Season with pepper.

2. In a large heavy skillet melt the butter over medium heat. Add the eggs and cook, stirring frequently, for 2 minutes. Stir in the lox and cook until the eggs are just set but not dry.

3. Place the muffin halves on individual plates. Spoon eggs onto each muffin and serve.

POTTER: So, how come you wound up in the foxhole?

SIDNEY FREEDMAN: Doing a follow-up. You can't just send them out and forget about them.

B.J.: Sidney, just think how much good you could do if you had a tank with a couch in it.

BREAKFAST

This is a great picture of Captain "Hawkeye" Pierce, Max Klinger, Colonel Blake, Radar, and Captain "Trapper" McIntrye. They're waitin' for me to bring them some spareribs Captain Pierce had delivered all the way from Home!

"There's pudding in the pillow."
—HOT LIPS

Trapper's Trapped Eggs

Serves 4 to 6

16	slices white bread, crusts removed
8	thin slices Canadian bacon
1/3	cup shredded Monterey Jack cheese
1/3	cup shredded Cheddar cheese
6	large eggs, beaten
1/2	teaspoon dry mustard
1/2	teaspoon salt
1/4	cup minced onions
1/4	cup chopped red bell pepper
1/2	cup unsalted butter, melted
1	cup crushed potato chips

1. On the bottom of a 9 x 13-inch baking pan place 8 slices of bread. On top of each slice of bread place a slice of Canadian bacon, then evenly sprinkle on the cheeses and top with another slice of bread. Combine the eggs, mustard, salt, onions, and bell pepper, and pour over the bread. Cover and refrigerate overnight.

2. In the morning, preheat the oven to 350°.

3. Pour the melted butter over the top, then evenly sprinkle on the potato chips. Bake for 1 hour. Serve.

IGORISM:
See those fresh oranges? They don't grow on trees, you know.

POLICE ACTION PANCAKES

Blake's Cakes with Cider Syrup

Makes about twenty-four 4-inch cakes

For the Syrup:

1	cup sugar
2	tablespoons cornstarch
½	teaspoon pumpkin pie spice
2	cups apple cider
2	tablespoons fresh lemon juice
¼	cup butter, melted

1. In a medium saucepan combine the sugar, cornstarch, and spice. Add the cider and lemon juice and cook over high heat, stirring constantly, until the mixture thickens and boils for 1 minute.

2. Remove from heat and stir in the melted butter.

For the Pancakes:

2	cups baking mix
½	teaspoon ground cinnamon
1	egg
1⅓	cups milk
¾	cup grated apples or applesauce

1. In a large bowl combine the baking mix, cinnamon, egg, and milk and beat until smooth. Fold in the apples.

2. Preheat a large skillet or griddle. Test the griddle by dropping on a few drops of cold water. If the water bounces and sizzles, the griddle is ready.

3. Pour ¼ cup for each pancake onto the hot griddle. In 2 or 3 minutes the cake surfaces should begin to bubble. Lift each cake with a spatula to check the underside. When they are golden brown flip the pancakes once and cook until the opposite side has browned.

4. Transfer the hot pancakes to individual plates and serve with Cider Syrup.

Blake, Burns, and Radar.

Frontline Flapjacks with Chocolate Gravy

Makes about ten 4-inch cakes

For the Gravy:

1	cup sugar
1/8	teaspoon salt
2	tablespoons all-purpose flour
3	tablespoons unsweetened cocoa
1	cup water
1	teaspoon vanilla extract

1. In a large saucepan mix the dry ingredients together. Gradually add the water.

2. While stirring constantly, heat the mixture slowly to a boil. As the gravy thickens, remove from the heat and continue to stir constantly. Mix in the vanilla.

For the Pancakes:

1	cup all-purpose flour
3/4	teaspoon baking powder
1/2	teaspoon baking soda
1/2	teaspoon salt
1	teaspoon sugar
1	cup buttermilk
1	egg, beaten until light
2	tablespoons unsalted butter, melted

1. Into a large mixing bowl sift together all of the dry ingredients. Add the buttermilk, egg, and butter, mixing until just blended. Do not overmix; lumps are OK.

2. Preheat a large skillet or griddle. Test the griddle by dropping on a few drops of cold water. If the water bounces and sizzles, the griddle is ready.

3. Pour about ¼ cup of batter for each pancake onto a hot griddle. In 2 or 3 minutes the cake surfaces should begin to bubble. Lift each cake with a spatula to check the underside. When they are golden brown flip the pancakes once and cook until the opposite side has browned. Repeat with the remaining batter.

4. Serve immediately with butter and chocolate gravy.

Variation: Serve chocolate gravy over homemade buttermilk biscuits.

Majors Houlihan, Burns, Colonel Blake, and Radar doin' soldier stuff.

BREAKFAST

That's me takin' a quiz to get a promotion.

Here are the Dr.'s givin' me my test for a promotion. I didn't get one.

Hangover Pancakes

Makes about twenty-four 4-inch cakes

2	cups baking mix
2	tablespoons sugar
½	teaspoon ground cinnamon
⅛	teaspoon grated nutmeg
5	eggs, beaten
½	cup beer
2	tablespoons vegetable oil

1. In a large bowl combine the dry ingredients. In a medium bowl combine the eggs, beer, and oil and mix well. Add the liquid mixture to the dry ingredients, mixing with a fork until just blended. Do not overmix; lumps are OK.

2. Preheat a large skillet or griddle. Test the griddle by dropping on a few drops of cold water. If the water bounces and sizzles, the griddle is ready.

3. Pour about ¼ cup of batter for each pancake onto the griddle. In 2 or 3 minutes the cake surfaces should begin to bubble. Lift each cake with a spatula to check the underside. When they are golden brown flip the pancakes once and cook until the opposite side has browned. Repeat with the remaining batter. Serve hot.

"Hey, B.J., wake up. The sun is shining. The birds are twittering. What a breakfast. Poached sludge."
—HAWKEYE

Dear Ma,

Katherine (I call her Kat), one of the nurses here, just got a package of cheeses from her father, Tony, in Brooklyn. Gorgonzola and ricotta she calls' em. Ma, I've never seen stuff like this. The gorgonzola smells awful but tastes really good. I'm gonna try to make a sauce and pour it over Colonel Potter's pork chops. It's funny, I thought all cheese came in little flat, yellow squares.

Love, Igor

BREAKFAST

Hockey Puck Pancakes

Makes about twenty-four 4-inch cakes

2	eggs
2	tablespoons sugar
¾	cup whole milk
¼	cup vegetable oil
2⅓	cups baking mix
8	slices bacon, fried and crumbled

1. In a large bowl beat the eggs with an electric mixer on high speed for 5 minutes, or until thick and lemon-colored. Add the remaining ingredients and mix well.

2. Preheat a large skillet or griddle. Test the griddle by dropping on a few drops of cold water. If the water bounces and sizzles, the griddle is ready.

3. Pour about ¼ cup of batter for each pancake onto the griddle. In 2 or 3 minutes the cake surfaces should begin to bubble. Lift each cake with a spatula to check the underside. When they are golden brown flip the pancakes once and cook until the opposite side has browned. Repeat with the remaining batter. Serve hot.

The nurses' quarters.

Colonel Potter's Pottage

Serves 6

2	tablespoons unsalted butter
1	large yellow onion, diced
2	cups chopped and seeded tomatoes
2	cups cooked oatmeal
3	carrots, cooked and sliced
1	quart water
1	cup cooked split peas
⅛	teaspoon salt

1. In a large pot over medium-high heat melt the butter. Add the onion and cook until browned.
2. Add the remaining ingredients and cook for 20 minutes. Serve.

"Boy, these eggs are bland. I think they threw away the eggs and scrambled the cartons."
—COLONEL POTTER

M*A*S*H Mush

Serves 2 to 4

1½   cups water

¼   cup raisins

½   fresh apple, peeled and coarsley chopped

¼   teaspoon salt

¾   cup regular oats

1   pinch fresh grated nutmeg

      Ground cinnamon

1. In a medium saucepan bring the water, raisins, and apple to a boil. Add the salt and nutmeg, then slowly stir in the oats. Cook over medium low to medium heat for about 5 minutes until the oatmeal is thick.

2. Transfer to individual serving bowls and sprinkle each with a little ground cinnamon.

Here's a shot of Colonel Potter, Captain Pierce, and Major Houlihan wondering what's for breakfast.

Nurse Kellye's Coffee Cake Cure

Serves 4 to 6

For the Cake:

1⅓   cups all-purpose flour

1⅓   cups regular or quick-cooking oats

½   teaspoon salt

2   teaspoons baking powder

⅔   cup firmly packed dark brown sugar

     Grated zest of 2 oranges

2   eggs, lightly beaten

1   cup milk

⅔   cup vegetable oil

1. Preheat the oven to 350°.
2. In a large mixing bowl combine the flour, oats, salt, baking powder, and brown sugar. Add the orange zest, eggs, milk, and oil and mix well. Pour the mixture into an ungreased 7 x 12-inch baking pan.

For the Topping:

⅓   cup firmly packed raw brown sugar

½   cup chopped walnuts

2   tablespoons all-purpose flour

1   teaspoon ground cinnamon

2   tablespoons butter, melted

In a small bowl combine the topping ingredients. Sprinkle on top of the cake mixture just before baking. Bake for 30 minutes.

Father Mulcahy, Captain Hunnicut and Nurse Kellye find a delicious morsel.

FRANK: That's a dog! I'm not going to operate on a dumb dog!
RADAR: C'mon sir, dogs are people too.

Operation Oatmeal

Serves 6 to 8

½   cup unsalted butter, melted

1   cup firmly packed brown sugar

2   eggs, beaten

½   teaspoon salt

2   teaspoons baking powder

1   cup milk

3   cups quick-cooking oats

1. Preheat the oven to 350°. Grease an 8 x 8-inch baking pan.

2. In a large mixing bowl combine the ingredients one by one in the order given. Pour the mixture into the pan and spread evenly. Bake for 45 minutes.

3. Serve cut in squares as a breakfast bar or as a dessert spooned into a bowl and topped with warm fresh or canned fruit, topped with cold milk.

A day on the chopper pad.

BREAKFAST

Tent Post Toast

Serves 2 to 3

1	16-ounce can stewed tomatoes
	Salt and pepper to taste
1	tablespoon Worcestershire sauce
⅛	teaspoon Tabasco sauce
1½	tablespoons butter
6	slices white bread, toasted

1. In a medium mixing bowl combine the tomatoes, salt, pepper, Worcestershire sauce, and Tabasco.

2. In a medium saucepan melt the butter over medium heat. Add the tomato mixture to the melted butter and simmer for about 3 minutes.

3. Pour tomatoes over the toast and serve.

The good old mess tent.

The Colonel is checkin' up on poor sick Igor.

FRANK: Hello, Major. May I join you for some pleasant conversation?

HOT LIPS: Of course, Frank. Sit down and keep your mouth shut.

BREAKFAST

Uncle Ed's Oatmeal Shake

Makes about 6 1-cup servings

2	cups cooked oatmeal
1	medium ripe banana
4	cups water
2	tablespoons honey
½	teaspoon salt

1. Combine all of the ingredients in a blender and mix until smooth.
2. Chill and serve.

We have some fun here sometimes.

The nurses rush to the chopper pad.

The nurses come home.

BREAKFAST

UN Troop Toast

with Sautéed Apples and Pecans

Serves 4

4	large eggs, lightly beaten
1	cup milk
2	tablespoons light rum
1½	teaspoons vanilla extract
¼	teaspoon salt
8	1-inch thick French bread slices
6	tablespoons butter
2	apples, peeled, cored, and chopped
½	teaspoon ground cinnamon
3	ounces pecans, chopped
½	cup crushed pineapple
½	cup water
¼	cup firmly packed brown sugar

1. In a medium bowl whisk together the eggs, milk, rum, vanilla, and salt. In a shallow dish place the bread slices in a single layer. Pour the egg mixture over the bread and let stand for 15 minutes or until the egg mixture is absorbed, turning occasionally with a spatula.

2. In a large heavy skillet melt 4 tablespoons of butter over medium heat. Add the apples, season with cinnamon, and sauté for 5 minutes. Add the pecans and sauté for 5 minutes. Add the crushed pineapple, water, and brown sugar and cook, stirring constantly, for 5 minutes or until the mixture has thickened and heated through. Remove from the heat and set aside.

3. In a large heavy skillet melt the remaining 2 tablespoons of butter over medium heat. Cook the bread on each side until brown and slightly crisp. Add more butter if needed until all the bread is cooked. Transfer to individual plates, spoon the apple-pecan mixture over the toast, and serve.

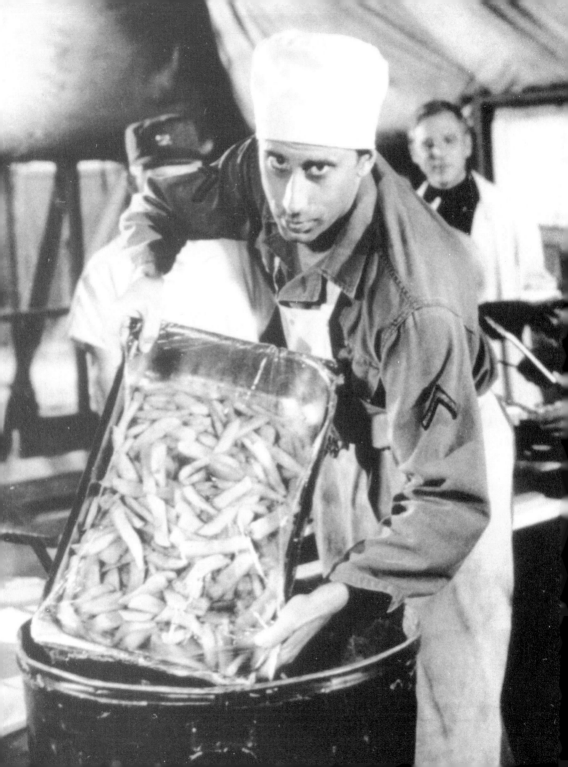

• LUNCH •

Cream of Weenie Soup

Serves 4 to 6

¼	cup unsalted butter
1	tablespoon fresh chopped garlic
1	cup chopped yellow onion
1	cup finely chopped carrots
1	cup diced potatoes (½-inch cubes)
1	cup finely diced celery
¼	cup all-purpose flour
1	cup chicken broth
½	cup dry sherry
⅛	teaspoon leaf tarragon
¼	teaspoon paprika
¼	teaspoon leaf thyme
¼	teaspoon ground white pepper
2	plum tomatoes, cored, seeded, and cut into ½-inch strips
1	cup half and half
4	weenies, cut into ½-inch slices
1	cup cooked crumbled bacon
1	tablespoon chopped fresh parsley

1. In a large sauté pan melt the butter over medium-high heat. Add the garlic, onions, carrots, potatoes, and celery and sauté for 3 minutes. Blend in the flour and cook for 3 minutes. Add the chicken broth, sherry, and all of the seasonings and bring to a boil. Add the tomatoes, half and half, weenies, and bacon, reduce the heat, and simmer for 10 minutes until the mixture thickens.

2. Ladle into individual soup bowls and garnish with chopped parsley.

That's me and Roy just before Captain Pierce started yellin' about the liver and the fish.

FLAGG: And get me a box of scorpions as well.
RADAR: Scorpions, as in scorpions?
FLAGG: Big ones.
HAWKEYE: What the hell are you going to do with
a box of scorpions?
FLAGG: Gift for a friend.

Creamed Green

Serves 4

2	cups water
1	pound fresh spinach, washed well and stems removed
1	clove garlic, minced
¼	cup prepared Hollandaise sauce
1	tablespoon butter, softened
4	slices cooked bacon, crumbled

1. In a large saucepan bring the water to a boil. Add the spinach, reduce the heat, and simmer for about 6 minutes or until tender. Drain the spinach well and discard the water.

2. Transfer the spinach to a blender or food processor. Add the garlic, Hollandaise sauce, and butter and blend briefly. Return the mixture to the saucepan and heat through. Serve immediately with crumbled bacon sprinkled on top.

Here's a bunch of my friends in the mess tent.

They posed just for you, Ma!

KLINGER:
Why do I always get stuck
between a rock and a hard place?

IGOR;
I just serve this slop—
I don't explain it.

LUNCH

Creamy Veggie Soup

Serves 6 to 8

1	tablespoon olive oil
1	large yellow onion, chopped
3	medium sweet potatoes, peeled and chopped
3	medium zucchini, chopped
1	bunch broccoli, chopped
1	clove garlic, minced
2	quarts chicken broth
2	medium russet potatoes, peeled and shredded
1	to 2 teaspoons ground cumin
1	teaspoon salt
½	teaspoon pepper
1	tablespoon butter
2	cups light cream (or 1 can evaporated skim milk)

1. In a large kettle heat the olive oil over medium-high heat. Add the onion and sauté until slightly browned. Add the sweet potatoes, zucchini, broccoli, and garlic and sauté for 4 to 5 minutes or until the vegetables are tender but crisp.

2. Stir in the broth and bring to a simmer. Add the potatoes and seasonings and cook for 8 to 10 minutes or until the vegetables are tender and the shredded potatoes break down and thicken the broth. Stir in the butter and cream, heat through, and serve.

> **IGORISM:**
> I can't smell anymore, Colonel. I been here too long.

Dear Ma,

Get this, one day I started heating up a pan I was gonna fry a piece of fish in, when all of a sudden I remember it's time to check all the rat traps. It took me at least ten minutes, or more, to clean and reset. Anyway, I came back, put a bunch of pepper and stuff on the fish and threw it in the pan. Holy moly, Ma, that pan got so hot that it burned one side of the fish almost black in just a few seconds. I quickly tried to get it out of the pan, but it just flipped over and burned on the other side, too. Here's the funny part — and don't think I'm crazy — the fish tasted great! I'm gonna burn every piece I eat from now on! Ha ha. You should invite Norma over for dinner and try this. Don't forget the secret: light a fire under the pan, go check your traps, and you're ready to cook.

Love, Igor

LUNCH

Igor's Caustic Chili Corn Pudding

Serves 4 to 6

1	15½-ounce can creamed corn
2	eggs, beaten
1	cup yellow cornmeal
½	teaspoon baking soda
¾	cup buttermilk
1	cup (2 sticks) butter, melted
2	cups grated sharp Cheddar cheese
3	chili peppers (at least), minced (a combination of red and green for color)

1. Preheat the oven to 350°. Grease a 9 x 9-inch baking pan.

2. In a large mixing bowl combine the corn, eggs, cornmeal, baking soda, buttermilk, and melted butter and mix well. Pour half of the batter into the prepared pan. Add half of the Cheddar cheese in an even layer, then sprinkle chilies on top of the cheese. Add the remaining cheese and pour the remaining batter on top. Bake for 1 hour.

3. Remove from the oven and cool for 15 minutes. Cut into squares and serve.

Father Mulcahy asked me to take down some
mighty nice artwork in the Officer's Club.

LUNCH

Sorry 'Bout That Father Creamed Corn

Serves 4

2	cups fresh corn kernels (cut from 3 to 4 ears of corn)
¾	cup heavy cream
1	teaspoon Worcestershire sauce
	Salt and pepper to taste
2	cloves garlic, minced
3	tablespoons unsalted butter

1. Preheat the oven to 325°. Generously butter a 9 x 9-inch baking pan.

2. In a large mixing bowl combine all of the ingredients except the butter. Pour the mixture into the prepared baking pan. Dot the top with butter. Bake for 1 hour.

I didn't know Father Mulcahy wanted me to leave the corn on his darn ol' cobs.

Gooey Grenades

Chili-Cheese Stuffed French Rolls

Serves 12

4	cups shredded Cheddar cheese
1	medium onion, finely chopped
1	7-ounce can diced green chilies
1	2¼-ounce can (drained weight) chopped black olives, drained
1	8-ounce can tomato sauce
¼	cup vegetable oil
2	tablespoons white vinegar
2	tablespoons Worcestershire sauce
	Garlic salt to taste
12	medium French rolls

1. Preheat the oven to 350°.

2. In a large bowl combine the Cheddar, onion, chilies, olives, tomato sauce, vegetable oil, vinegar, Worcestershire sauce, and garlic salt, and mix thoroughly.

3. Cut the rolls about one third from the top and scoop out the larger section. Fill each bread shell with a generous spoonful of the cheese mixture, and put its little top back on.

4. Wrap each grenade in tin foil and place on a baking sheet. Bake for 35 minutes or until the cheese mixture is completely melted. Serve hot.

LUNCH

Captain Pierce is all excited about puttin' that piece of toast into a thing he called a time capsule. Don't know why he'd want to save toast.

I work in the Officer's Club, too!

Igor's Seizure Salad Sandwich

Serves 4 to 6

¾   cup Great Caesar's Salad Dressing (see recipe, page 60)

½   cup sun-dried tomatoes

1   14-ounce loaf Italian bread

1   head romaine lettuce, outer leaves discarded, then washed, dried ,and chilled

¾   pound cooked turkey breast, very coarsely chopped

3   ounces Parmesan cheese, shaved thinly

Salt and freshly ground pepper to taste

1. Prepare the Caesar Dressing and set aside.

2. Preheat the oven to 350°.

3. Bring a small saucepan of water to a boil. Add the sun-dried tomatoes and blanch for 2 to 3 minutes. Drain and let cool. Slice each tomato in half and reserve.

4. Cut the loaf of bread in half lengthwise and remove most of the soft inner bread. Brush the bread shells with a little Caesar Dressing. Place on a baking sheet inside up and bake for 5 minutes or until golden brown.

5. In a large bowl add mainly small crisp inner romaine leaves, turkey, Parmesan, tomatoes and the remaining dressing. Toss to coat well. Spoon the salad into the bottom half of the bread, season with salt and pepper, then top with the other half. Slice crosswise into desired portions and serve.

LUNCH

Officers' Club Sandwich

Grilled Bacon, Tomato, and Jack Sandwiches

Serves 4

10	slices bacon, cooked and crumbled
8	ounces Monterey Jack cheese, grated
1	small jalapeño pepper, minced
1½	teaspoons mayonnaise
1	tablespoon Dijon mustard
¼	cup unsalted butter
2	cloves garlic, minced
1	16-inch loaf French bread, cut diagonally into 8 slices
1	large plum tomato, cut into 4 slices

1. Preheat the broiler.

2. In a medium bowl combine the bacon, Monterey Jack cheese, jalapeño pepper, mayonnaise, and mustard and mix well.

3. In a small saucepan melt the butter and sauté the garlic for 1 minute. Brush the garlic butter on one side of each of the bread slices. Spread the bacon-cheese mixture over 4 of the slices on the unbuttered side, and place 1 tomato slice on top of each.

4. In a large ovenproof skillet over medium-high heat grill the sandwich halves and the tops buttered side down until they start to brown.

5. Transfer to the broiler just until the tomatoes soften. Remove and place the top halves on. Transfer to individual plates and serve.

LUNCH

"Old Bird" Sandwiches with Orange Sauce

Hot Turkey and Asparagus Sandwiches with Cheddar Sauce

Serves 4

Cheddar Cheese Sauce:

1	tablespoon unsalted butter
2	tablespoons all-purpose flour
¾	cup milk
¼	teaspoon Worcestershire sauce
¼	teaspoon prepared mustard
	Salt and pepper to taste
1	cup shredded sharp Cheddar cheese

1. In a small saucepan melt the butter over medium heat. Stir in the flour. Blend in the milk, Worcestershire sauce, mustard, salt, and pepper. Stir until the mixture is well blended and smooth. Continue to stir while cooking until the mixture thickens and boils.

2. Remove from the heat, add the Cheddar cheese, and stir until smooth. Cover and set aside.

For the Sandwiches:

1	10-ounce package frozen asparagus spears
8	thick diagonal slices Italian bread
1	7-ounce jar roasted red peppers, drained
8	ounces cooked turkey breast, sliced

LUNCH

1. Preheat the oven to 375°.

2. Cook the asparagus according to the package instructions. Drain and rinse in cold water to stop cooking.

3. Place the bread slices on a baking sheet. Divide the red peppers among the bread slices. Cover with turkey slices and top with asparagus. Spoon Cheddar sauce over the asparagus and bake for 8 minutes or until heated through.

Hot Lips, I mean Major Houlihan, diggin' in some crab legs with the Colonel.

LUNCH

Radar and the Colonel don't seem to like what's under Klinger's coat.

Looks like the Colonel is gonna pick Klinger's nose—ha ha.

LUNCH

Shell-Shocked Crab and Cheese Bread

Serves 4

1	16-inch loaf French bread, cut in half lengthwise and hollowed out
10	ounces Gorgonzola cheese, crumbled
¼	cup mayonnaise
8	ounces cooked fresh crab meat, flaked and picked over for shell or filament
1	jalapeño pepper, minced
¼	cup grated Parmesan cheese

1. Preheat the oven to 350°.

2. Place the bread halves on an ungreased baking sheet. Sprinkle each with Gorgonzola. In a small bowl combine the mayonnaise, crab meat, and jalapeño pepper and mix well. Spoon the mixture over the cheese then sprinkle Parmesan on top.

3. Bake for 20 minutes. Cut each piece in half and serve.

After the fire.

Toasted Tank Tuna

Serves 4

1	14-ounce can water-packed white albacore tuna
½	cup mayonnaise
1	small carrot, peeled and chopped
⅛	teaspoon dried dill weed
⅛	teaspoon lemon pepper
1	tablespoon sweet pickle relish
1	tablespoon minced yellow onion
1	head romaine lettuce, washed, dried, coarsely chopped, and chilled
8	slices white bread, toasted

1. In a large bowl combine the tuna, mayonnaise, carrot, dill, lemon pepper, relish, and onion, and mix well.

2. Place some chopped lettuce on 4 toast slices and top with a generous amount of the tuna mixture. Top with toast slices, cut in half diagonally, and serve.

That smile would make anybody feel better!

LUNCH

Tourniquet Turkey Melt

Serves 2

4	1-inch thick slices French bread, toasted
1	tablespoon pesto
1	tablespoon mayonnaise
½	pound cooked turkey breast, thinly sliced
1	plum tomato, thinly sliced
1	small red onion, thinly sliced (optional)
4	slices Provolone cheese, halved

1. Preheat the broiler.

2. Arrange the toasted French bread on a baking sheet. Combine the pesto and mayonnaise in a small bowl. Spread the mixture on the toast then top each with turkey, tomato, onion, and cheese.

3. Place 5 inches below the broiler for 3 to 5 minutes or until the cheese is melted and slightly browned.

Here's a nice shot of a hungry Major.

Dear Ma,

How are things back in the world? That's how we talk about home. Most of us feel so far away, it's like we're not even on the same planet. It can make you act a little goofy sometimes. Hawkeye (his father nicknamed him that from a character in a book), one of the smartest doctors here, went crazy in the chow line the other day. He made me nervous because he was lookin' at me real funny when I was about to give him his food. Now get this, I tell him for an entree he can have either liver or fish, and he goes nuts! He starts yellin' that he's eaten so much fish and liver he's gonna grow some gills, and that he can't do certain things without gettin' smothered in onions first! Ha ha. Then, for no reason, he throws all the food on his tray across the tent, jumps up on one of the mess tables and starts singing, "I-want-something-else!" Well, everybody in the Mess tent starts bangin' their spoons and stuff with him. My buddy, Roy, and me didn't know what else to do, so we started bangin' stuff too. He finally calmed down and went to the officers' club for pretzels. Don't think bad about him, Ma, he's a pretty nice guy who probably wouldn't do anything like that back in his world.

Love, Igor

LUNCH

Truman's Reubens

Serves 4

8   slices pumpernickel or other dark bread, toasted

1   pound corned beef, thinly sliced

1½   cups sauerkraut, drained

8   slices American cheese

     Mustard

¼   cup butter, melted

1. Top each of 4 slices of bread with ¼ pound of corned beef, one-fourth of the sauerkraut, and 2 slices of cheese. Spread one side of the remaining bread with mustard.

2. Brush the outsides of each sandwich with melted butter.

3. In a large skillet over medium-high heat grill each sandwich on both sides until the cheese is melted. Serve immediately.

I just found out that I'm comin' home.

Boomin' Black Bean Salad

Makes about 10 cups

3	15-ounce cans cooked black beans, about 6 cups
1	medium green bell pepper, finely chopped
1	medium red bell pepper, finely chopped
1	medium yellow bell pepper, finely chopped
2	medium plum tomatoes, seeded and finely chopped
2	bunches cilantro, finely chopped
2	stalks celery, finely chopped
4	green onions, finely chopped
¼	cup olive oil
2	tablespoons cider vinegar
4	chugs Worcestershire sauce
2	tablespoons ground cumin seed
1	teaspoon cayenne pepper
	Tabasco sauce to taste

1. Combine all of the ingredients in a large bowl and mix well. Transfer the mixture to a colander and let drain.

2. When thoroughly drained, discard the liquid and transfer the salad to a bowl. Cover and refrigerate for at least 2 hours before serving.

Variations: This can be eaten like a salad or spooned into some heated corn or flour tortillas or stuffed into pita bread pockets.

LUNCH

Bread Bullets

Cheese and Garlic Croutons

1	loaf day-old French bread, cut into 1-inch cubes
2	tablespoons olive oil
¼	cup grated Parmesan cheese
½	teaspoon basil
½	teaspoon oregano
½	teaspoon garlic salt
⅛	teaspoon pepper

1. Preheat the oven to 300°.

2. Place the bread in a large bowl. Sprinkle with olive oil and toss to coat evenly.

3. In small bowl combine the Parmesan cheese and seasonings. Sprinkle the mixture over the bread and mix until thoroughly coated.

4. Spread the croutons in a single layer on a baking sheet. Bake for 30 minutes until golden brown. Stir once or twice while baking to insure even browning. Remove from the oven and let cool. Use right away or store for future use in an airtight container.

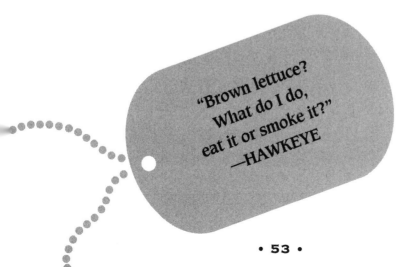

"Brown lettuce? What do I do, eat it or smoke it?"
—HAWKEYE

Brown Lettuce Salad

Romaine and Chopped Tomato Salad with Gorgonzola Vinaigrette Dressing

Serves 4 to 6

For the Tomatoes:

2	tablespoons balsamic vinegar
2	tablespoons olive oil
3	cloves garlic, minced
4	Roma tomatoes, seeded and chopped
	Salt and freshly ground black pepper to taste

In a medium bowl combine the vinegar, olive oil, and garlic. Add the tomatoes and toss to coat well. Season with salt and pepper, cover the bowl with plastic wrap, and refrigerate for 2 hours.

For the Dressing:

Makes ¾ cup

2	tablespoons balsamic vinegar
1	teaspoon Dijon mustard
¼	cup olive oil
¼	cup safflower oil
3	ounces Gorgonzola cheese, crumbled
	Salt and pepper to taste

In a medium bowl combine the vinegar and mustard and mix well. Add the oils and whisk until smooth. Add the cheese, salt, and pepper, mix well, and set aside.

For the Salad:

1   medium head romaine lettuce, washed, dried, chopped, and chilled

½   cup coarsely chopped watercress, stems removed

1   cup chopped mushrooms

In a large salad bowl combine the lettuce, watercress, and mushrooms. Drain the chopped tomatoes and add them to the salad. Add the dressing and toss well. Serve immediately.

POTTER: Fire the gun, Hawkeye.

HAWKEYE: Colonel, I'll treat their wounds. Heal their wounds. Bind their wounds. But I will not inflict their wounds.

POTTER: You can't just sit there.

HAWKEYE: I may be sitting on the outside. But I'm running on the inside.

Cease-Fire Salad

Serves 4 to 6

1	cup cooked green beans, chopped
1	cup cauliflower florets
1	medium zucchini, sliced
1	bunch green onions, chopped
8	cherry tomatoes, halved
1	4-ounce can black olives
¾	cup olive oil
1	large lemon, halved
2	tablespoons leaf oregano
	Salt and pepper to taste

1. Combine the vegetables, olives, and olive oil in a large bowl and mix well. Squeeze the fresh lemon halves over the salad, add the oregano, salt, and pepper and mix again. Cover and refrigerate for 1 hour.

2. Transfer to individual chilled salad plates and serve.

"They're getting younger every day. I don't know what's greener, them or their uniforms."
—IGOR

Combat-Ready Coleslaw

Serves 4 to 6

Roquefort Sour Cream Dressing:

2   ounces Roquefort or blue cheese

½   cup sour cream

1½   teaspoons white wine vinegar

Combine the Roquefort, sour cream, and vinegar in a blender and mix until smooth.

For the Coleslaw:

1   head green cabbage, chopped coarsely

1   cup seedless green grapes, halved

½   cup chopped walnuts

2   green onions, chopped

1   carrot, shredded

    Salt and pepper to taste

1   recipe Roquefort Sour Cream Dressing

Combine all of the ingredients in a large bowl and mix well. Cover and refrigerate for 1 hour. Serve chilled.

Major Burns got a little cranky with me about runnin' the projector.

I don't think he likes movies very much.

Private First Class Pasta Salad

Serves 2

For the Dressing:

¼	cup white wine vinegar
¼	cup olive oil
2	cloves garlic, minced
½	teaspoon basil
¼	teaspoon oregano
⅛	teaspoon black pepper

Combine the dressing ingredients and reserve.

For the Pasta:

8	ounces radiatore pasta
1	2½-ounce pepperoni stick, halved lengthwise, then cut into ¼-inch pieces
1	cup canned red kidney beans, drained
½	pound cherry tomatoes, halved
1	small red bell pepper, cut into 1-inch pieces
4	ounces Provolone cheese, cubed

1. Cook the pasta according to the package instructions and drain well.
2. In a large bowl combine the pasta, pepperoni, kidney beans, tomatoes, red bell pepper, and cheese. Add the dressing and toss well. Chill and serve.

LUNCH

Sherman's Great Caesar's Salad!

Serves 4

For the Dressing:

Makes about 2½ cups

3	eggs, coddled (or 2 Egg Beaters "eggs")
4	tablespoons white wine vinegar
3	cloves garlic, chopped
½	cup vegetable oil
1	tin anchovy fillets
½	cup olive oil
¼	cup grated Parmesan cheese

It is best to coddle the eggs (rather than using the traditional raw eggs) to eliminate any risk of salmonella poisoning. Or you can use Egg Beaters. They make a thicker dressing, so use the equivalent of 2 eggs.

1. For coddling: With a tablespoon, lower the unshelled eggs carefully into boiling water. Remove the pan from the heat and cover the pan. Let stand for 6 to 7 minutes.

2. Shell and transfer the eggs to the bowl of a food processor fitted with the steel blade. Add the remaining ingredients and process until smooth. Cover and refrigerate. Can be made 1 or 2 days in advance.

For the Salad:

1	head romaine lettuce, washed, dried, chopped and chilled
¼	cup grated Parmesan cheese
¼	cup grated Romano cheese
¾	cup Bread Bullets (see recipe, page 53)

LUNCH

⅓   cup pine nuts, toasted (bake at 350° for 10 minutes)
     Freshly ground black pepper

Place the chilled romaine in a large salad bowl. Add 1/2 to 3/4 cup Caesar dressing and toss well. Add the cheeses and toss, then add the croutons and toss. Add the pine nuts and plenty of black pepper, toss, and serve immediately.

Colonel Potter givin' Major Houlihan a ride on Sophie.

Dear Ma,

Remember me throwing up on Dr. Jaffee's nurse whenever I had to get a shot? Well, if I did that every time I got one over here, the nurses would be an awful mess! Ha ha. They all work really hard helping in the OR (operating room) and stuff. Don't ever tell I said this, but I think some of them work harder than the doctors. And please don't tell Janine, but I have a little crush on Major Houlihan who's in charge of all the nurses. That's MARGARET Houlihan — she's a she Major. They call her Hot Lips because, well, uh, anyway they do. One day I got this flu and the Major, herself, was gonna give me a shot for it. She always seemed kinda mean so I was really nervous about gettin' sick on her. Anyway, just before she sticks the needle in, she squeezes my hand, smiles this beautiful smile, and asks me where I'm from. Don't know exactly what it was, but I looked in her eyes and forgot all about throwin' up. Even while she was yellin' at me a couple of days later, all I could think about was her smile. Can't wait for my next flu. Just kidding! Ha ha.

Love, Igor

Shrapnel Salad

Hot Corn Salad

Serves 4 to 6

3	tablespoons olive oil
1	red onion, chopped
1	cup fresh corn kernels, cut from 1 to 2 ears of corn
1	bunch endive, shredded
1	red bell pepper, seeded and julienned
1	yellow bell pepper, seeded and julienned
6	strips bacon, cooked and chopped
½	cup rice vinegar

1. In a wok or sauté pan heat the olive oil over high heat. Add all of the ingredients and stir-fry for 30 to 60 seconds.
2. Transfer to a bowl and serve immediately.

The posh latrine.

LUNCH

Side-Arm Shell Salad

with Anchovy Vinaigrette

Serves 4

For the Dressing:

⅓   cup extra-virgin olive oil

¼   cup red wine vinegar

¼   teaspoon Dijon mustard

¼   teaspoon anchovy paste (or 1 anchovy fillet, finely chopped)

¼   teaspoon salt

⅛   teaspoon black pepper

⅛   teaspoon sugar

In a jar with a tight-fitting lid combine all of the above ingredients. Shake the contents vigorously for 1 minute and serve. If made in advance, refrigerate. Shake well before using.

For the Salad:

5   medium heads Belgian endive, separated, washed, dried, and chilled

2   ripe avocados, peeled, pitted, and cut into ¼-inch slices then coated with lemon juice to prevent browning

2   medium plum tomatoes, seeded and diced

⅛   teaspoon salt

¼   teaspoon freshly ground black pepper

6   fresh basil leaves, chopped

¼   purple onion, thinly sliced then halved

½   pound large cooked shrimp, peeled, deveined, and sliced in half lengthwise

1   fresh lemon, halved

¼   pound cooked crawfish or lobster chopped into ½ inch pieces

3   ounces feta cheese, crumbled

1. On a large round platter, place the large outer endive leaves points out, in a circular pattern. Place an avocado slice on each of the leaves. Sprinkle diced tomatoes over the avocado. Season with salt and pepper and sprinkle with basil.

2. Distribute the onion evenly over the tomatoes, then place the shrimp uniformly over the onions. Drizzle lemon juice over the shrimp.

3. Place the endive centers and pieces in the center of the platter, top with crawfish, and drizzle with lemon juice. Finally, sprinkle feta over the shrimp. Serve with dressing on the side and slices of crusty French bread.

This salad can be prepared up to several hours ahead. Cover and refrigerate until serving.

Major Houlihan reads 'em the rules.

I made a nice candlelit dinner for Captain Pierce and his date.

IGOR SPECIALS

Back-in-the-World Cabbage Soup

Serves 6 to 8

1	pound lean ground beef
1	large yellow onion, chopped
2	cloves garlic, chopped
2	large carrots, sliced
3	cups chopped cabbage
2	16-ounce cans whole tomatoes, chopped
2	cups water
1	beef bouillon cube
1	cup long grain rice
2	teaspoons Worcestershire sauce
2	tablespoons firmly packed brown sugar
2	teaspoons fresh lemon juice
¼	teaspoon leaf basil
¼	teaspoon leaf oregano
	Salt and pepper to taste

1. In a large heavy pot sauté the beef, onion, garlic, and carrots over medium-high heat until the beef is completely browned.

2. Add the remaining ingredients and bring to a boil. Reduce the heat and simmer, stirring occasionally, for 30 minutes or until the rice is cooked and the vegetables are tender.

LUNCH

Chopper Chili

Serves 4 to 6

1	pound ground turkey
1	large yellow onion, chopped
1	green bell pepper, chopped
2	cloves garlic, minced
2	15-ounce cans white beans (northern, cannellini, or any combination of white beans)
2	15-ounce cans tomatoes, chopped, 1 can not drained
2	tablespoons chili powder
½	to 1 teaspoon cayenne pepper
1	teaspoon salt

1. In a large nonstick saucepan sauté the turkey, onion, green bell pepper, and garlic until the turkey is no longer pink and the onion is translucent. Add the remaining ingredients and simmer for 30 minutes.

Serve with Igor's Caustic Chili Corn Pudding (see recipe, page 38).

> "Tell the General I would offer him dinner, but as a doctor
> it's not for me to endanger his health."
> —B.J.

Chopper Suey

Serves 4 to 6

1	recipe Dress White Rice (see recipe, page 150)
3	tablespoons vegetable oil
1	cup chopped onions
2	cups chopped celery
1	cup chopped mushrooms
1	pound cooked pork, chicken, or beef, diced
2	cups bean sprouts
1	cup beef broth
¼	cup soy sauce
1	teaspoon sugar
2	teaspoons salt
	Chow Mein noodles for garnish

1. Prepare Dress White Rice according to the recipe directions.

2. In a deep heavy skillet heat the oil over medium-high heat. Sauté the onion and celery for about 3 minutes. Add the mushrooms, meat, and bean sprouts and continue to sauté for 2 to 3 minutes longer.

3. Add the beef broth, soy sauce, sugar, and salt and heat through.

4. Transfer the rice to a platter. Pour Chopper Suey over the rice and sprinkle with Chow Mein noodles. Serve immediately.

IGORISM:
Soup. Cream of weenie.

The Colonel's Kernel Stew

Serves 4

3   tablespoons unsalted butter

¾   cup finely diced yellow onion

4   cloves garlic, minced

1   large red bell pepper, seeded and diced

1   large green bell pepper, seeded and diced

¼   teaspoon dried red pepper flakes

½   teaspoon paprika

¾   teaspoon cayenne pepper

2   cups milk

1   cup low-sodium chicken stock

2   large russet potatoes, scrubbed and diced large

4   ears fresh white corn, kernels cut from the cob

      Salt and fresh ground pepper to taste

2   pounds medium uncooked shrimp, shelled and deveined

1. In a large saucepan melt the butter over medium-high heat. Add the onion and garlic and sauté for 2 minutes. Add the red and green bell peppers and sauté for 1 minute. Add the pepper flakes, paprika, and cayenne pepper and sauté until well mixed. Add the milk, chicken stock, potatoes, and corn and season with salt and pepper. Bring to a boil briefly, then reduce heat, cover and simmer, stirring occasionally, for about 25 minutes or until the potatoes are tender.

2. Add the shrimp and cook for 3 to 5 minutes or until they just turn opaque. Be careful not to overcook the shrimp. Ladle generous portions into individual bowls. Serve immediately with crusty bread.

LUNCH

Company Clerk Quiche

Serves 4

1½   cups milk

½   cup baking mix

6   tablespoons butter, at room temperature

3   eggs

⅛   teaspoon salt

1   cup chopped ham, chicken, or shrimp

¾   cup grated Gruyère or Cheddar cheese

1. Preheat the oven to 350°.

2. In the bowl of a food processor fitted with a steel blade combine the milk, baking mix, butter, eggs, and salt and process until well-blended.

3. Pour the batter into an ungreased 9- or 10-inch quiche or pie pan. Sprinkle on the meat and cheese and press down into the batter. Bake for 45 minutes. Remove and let cool for 10 minutes before serving.

Radar's goin' home. Lucky guy!

LUNCH

Creamed Weenies

Serves 4

1	8-ounce package weenies
5	tablespoons unsalted butter
1	medium onion, chopped
¼	cup all-purpose flour
2	cups milk
1	cup heavy cream
3	egg yolks
⅛	teaspoon grated nutmeg
	Salt and pepper to taste
¼	cup grated Parmesan cheese
1	14-ounce package spinach, cooked and drained well

1. Preheat the oven to 450°. Bake the weenies for 10 minutes.

2. In a medium-size sauté pan melt 1 tablespoon of butter and sauté the onion until soft but not brown.

3. Add and melt 4 tablespoons of butter until foaming. Blend in the flour and cook over low heat for 3 minutes.

4. Whisk in the milk and cream, gradually, to avoid lumping. Continue stirring with a wooden spoon until smooth.

5. In a small bowl combine the egg yolks with a little of the sauce and beat lightly. Pour the egg yolk mixture into the sauce, beating constantly. Add the nutmeg, salt, and pepper and continue cooking over low heat for 2 to 3 minutes until the sauce thickens. Add the grated Parmesan, spinach, and weenies and serve.

LUNCH

Servin' good creamed weenies always makes me smile.

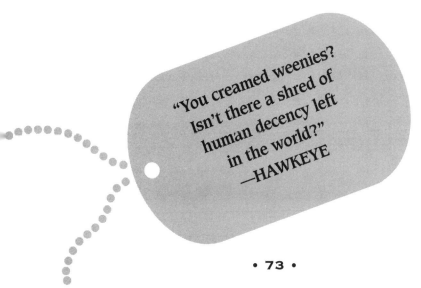

"You creamed weenies?
Isn't there a shred of
human decency left
in the world?"
—HAWKEYE

LUNCH

Drunken Crab Cakes

Makes six 3-inch cakes

Tequila Chili Sauce:

1	tablespoon mayonnaise
3	tablespoons Heinz chili sauce
2	tablespoons chopped cilantro
1	tablespoon tequila
½	teaspoon salt
½	teaspoon pepper
¼	cup safflower oil

In a small bowl combine all of the ingredients except the oil. Then, whisking constantly, pour in the oil and blend well. Serve or cover and refrigerate.

Crab Cakes:

1	egg, beaten
1	cup breadcrumbs
2	tablespoons grated Parmesan cheese
½	cup mayonnaise
1	large jalapeño pepper, chopped
2	tablespoons chopped parsley
1	teaspoon Worcestershire sauce
1	teaspoon basil
¼	teaspoon dry mustard
¼	teaspoon salt
½	teaspoon black pepper

1   pound fresh crab meat, picked over for shell or filament

2   tablespoons unsalted butter

1. In a medium mixing bowl combine the egg, ¾ cup breadcrumbs, Parmesan, mayonnaise, jalapeño pepper, parsley, Worcestershire sauce, basil, dry mustard, salt, and black pepper. Gently fold in the crab meat.

2. Shape the mixture into six 3-inch cakes. Coat the cakes with the remaining ¼ cup of breadcrumbs. Cover and refrigerate for 1 hour.

3. In a large skillet melt the butter over medium-high heat. Quickly brown the cakes on both sides. Reduce the heat and cook for about 6 minutes. Serve with Tequila Chili Sauce.

That's Rizzo lookin' at my grenade before I made it into your lamp.

Frank's Fussy Fritta

Fresh Tomato Basil Fritta Bruschetta

Serves 2 to 4

For the Bruschetta:

4	plum tomatoes, cored and coarsely chopped
2	tablespoons chopped fresh basil
1	teaspoon chopped fresh rosemary
1	tablespoon minced fresh garlic
3	dashes Tabasco sauce
⅛	teaspooon Cajun seasoning

In a medium bowl combine all of the ingredients and reserve.

For the Fritta:

4	ounces angel hair pasta (capelli d'angelo), broken or cut into 2-inch pieces
6	eggs, whipped well
1	tablespoon grated Parmesan cheese
	Salt and pepper to taste

1. Cook the angel hair according to the package instructions. Drain well.

2. Combine the eggs, pasta, Parmesan, salt, and pepper and mix well. Add the mixture to a nonstick omelette pan and cook over medium-high heat until the bottom is light brown, then place 8 inches under the broiler for 2 minutes or until the top of the omelet turns golden brown.

For the Garlic Toast:

1   tablespoon minced garlic
2   tablespoons olive oil
1   loaf Italian bread (large in diameter), cut in ¾-inch slices from the middle
       of the loaf

Preheat the broiler. Combine the garlic and oil, and brush over one side of each slice of bread.

To Make the Bruschetta:

Toast the bread lightly under the broiler. Transfer to individual plates and top with a portion of the fritta. Spoon the bruschetta generously over the fritta and serve.

Ma, this is Major Burns being friendly.

Gooey Green

Baked Spinach and Feta Cheese

Serves 4 to 6

4	10-ounce packages frozen chopped spinach
½	cup chopped yellow onion
4	ounces feta cheese, crumbled
¼	cup heavy cream
2	eggs, beaten
2	tablespoons butter, melted
2	teaspoons lemon juice
½	teaspoon pepper

1. Preheat the oven to 375°. Butter an 8 x 8-inch glass baking dish.

2. Cook the spinach according to the package instructions. Transfer to a colander, drain, and press out excess moisture. In a medium bowl combine the spinach and the remaining ingredients and mix well.

3. Transfer the spinach mixture to the prepared baking dish. Bake for 15 to 20 minutes and serve.

HAWKEYE:
I'll take some of
that orange stuff.

IGOR:
Ah, the
green beans.

Dear Ma,

The other day Major Burns picked me to fire a little cannon for a ceremonial salute. It was exciting until I realized that the cannon was pointed right at Radar who was playing his trumpet for the ceremony. I tried to tell the Major, but he ordered me to fire it anyway. And Ma, if you don't do something a Major orders you to do, it's a real bad thing. Anyway, I kinda shut my eyes and fired. Sure enough, Radar's head went flyin' right off his shoulders... Just kiddin'! Ha ha. The cannon ball missed his head but knocked the trumpet right out of his hands. I felt awful, but it's my job to follow orders even if they're lousy ones. Isn't that weird? Major Burns is such an odd duck that sometimes I feel a little sorry for him. I feel kinda sorry for the patients he operates on too. Ha ha.

Love, Igor

Helmet Hash

Serves 4

2	pounds sausage (cilantro turkey, smoked duck, or spicy chicken, etc.)
¼	cup olive oil
2	tablespoons minced fresh garlic
1½	cups diced yellow onion
1	cup chopped green onions
1	cup diced red bell pepper
1	cup diced green bell pepper
1	cup diced celery
1	cup chicken stock
2	cups cooked, diced, unpeeled red potatoes
1	teaspoon onion powder
½	teaspoon dry mustard
1	teaspoon paprika
1	teaspoon white pepper
1	tablespoon black pepper
	Cayenne pepper to taste

1. Preheat the oven to 450°. Bake the sausages for 10 minutes until brown. Let cool, then chop coarsely. Reduce the oven temperature to 350°.

2. In a large ovenproof skillet heat the olive oil. Add the garlic, onions, red and green peppers, and celery, and cook until tender.

3. Add the chicken stock, potatoes, sausage, and seasonings. Bake at 350° for 20 minutes. Let cool slightly before serving.

LUNCH

Igor's Cobless Corn Pudding

Serves 6 to 8

1	cup unbleached all-purpose flour
3	heaping teaspoons baking powder
⅓	cup sugar
¼	teaspoon salt
¼	teaspoon pepper
2	eggs, beaten
½	cup butter, melted
¼	cup milk
1	15¼-ounce can creamed corn
1¼	cups fresh corn kernels (about 2 ears)

1. Preheat the oven to 350°.

2. In a large mixing bowl combine the dry ingredients. Stir in the eggs, butter, milk, and canned corn, and mix thoroughly. Fold in the fresh corn.

3. Pour the batter into a greased 9 x 9-inch baking pan and bake for 25 to 30 minutes. Let cool slightly before serving.

"Igor, yours is a thankless task. So I hope you won't mind if I don't thank you."
—MULCAHY

P'Anmunjombalaya

Serves 4

2	tablespoons olive oil
¼	pound Andouille sausage, sliced diagonally into 1-inch pieces
1½	pounds chicken breasts, boned, skinned and cut into 1 x 2-inch strips
¼	cup chopped red bell pepper
¼	cup chopped green bell pepper
1	stalk celery, finely chopped
2	green onions, chopped
1	cup chicken broth
2	dashes Worcestershire sauce
4	dashes Tabasco sauce
1	teaspoon chopped fresh basil
1	teaspoon Cajun seasoning
⅛	teaspoon cayenne pepper
2	tablespoons minced fresh garlic
	Salt and pepper to taste
2	tablespoons prepared marinara sauce
1	cup chopped plum tomatoes
12	medium shrimp, shelled and deveined
2	cups hot cooked rice
1	fresh lemon, thinly sliced
1	tablespoon finely chopped fresh parsley
1	sprig fresh parsley

1. In a large sauté pan heat the olive oil over medium heat. Add the sausage, chicken, red and green bell peppers, celery, and onions and cook for 2 minutes. Then, add the chicken broth and all of the seasonings and spices and cook for 2

minutes. Add the marinara, tomatoes, and shrimp and cook for 3 minutes, turning the shrimp once. The shrimp should be pink and firm but not overcooked.

2. Spread the rice on a platter and pour jambalaya over the top, arranging the shrimp and chicken in a circular pattern. Garnish with halved lemon slices, chopped parsley, and the sprig of fresh parsley.

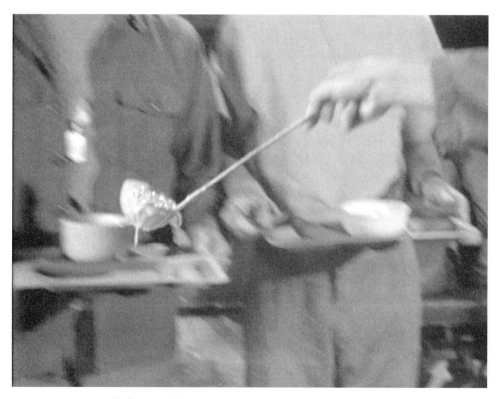

Over the liver and through the gums, look out stomach here it comes!

LUNCH

Post-Op Peppers and Beans
Serves 8

2	teaspoons salt
2	pounds fresh green beans, cut into 2-inch lengths
2	tablespoons olive oil
½	cup pine nuts
1	7-ounce jar roasted red peppers, drained and cut into 1-inch lengths
1	tablespoon chopped fresh basil
½	teaspoon fresh ground pepper

1. In a large pot bring 4 quarts of water to a boil. Add the salt and green beans and cook for 6 minutes or until tender. Drain and reserve.

2. In a large skillet heat the olive oil over medium heat. Add the pine nuts and sauté for 1 to 2 minutes. Add the roasted peppers, green beans, basil, and pepper and sauté until heated through.

Choppers!

Pressure Dropping Veggies

Serves 4

2   yellow crookneck squash, cut lengthwise into ¾-inch slices

4   Japanese eggplants, sliced lengthwise in half

1   large red bell pepper, stem and seeds removed and cut lengthwise into ¾-inch slices

¼   cup olive oil

Salt and freshly ground black pepper to taste

1. Preheat the barbecue grill on medium.

2. Brush both sides of the squash, eggplants, and bell pepper with olive oil. Season with salt and pepper. Barbecue for about 10 minutes on each side and serve.

I almost fell off a tent post to get this picture.

LUNCH

Radar's Teddy Bear Turkey Loaf

Serves 6

1¼	pounds ground turkey
¾	cup catsup
¾	cup oatmeal
1	medium onion, finely chopped
1	green bell pepper, chopped
8	cloves garlic, chopped
½	cup chopped fresh oregano
¼	cup Worcestershire sauce
	Salt and pepper to taste

1. Preheat the oven to 325°. Oil a 9-inch loaf pan. In a large bowl mix all of the ingredients. Transfer to the prepared pan and bake for 1 hour.

2. For a crusty top, increase the oven temperature to 450° and bake for 10 minutes longer. Allow to cool for 5 to 10 minutes to prevent crumbling. Serve warm or cool.

This is a picture of a bear and his friend Radar. Ha ha.

Tongue Depressing Baked Beans

Serves 6 to 8

1	pound dried white beans, soaked overnight in 6 cups of water
1	crumbled bay leaf
½	cup chopped yellow onion
½	pound salt pork, sliced
5	tablespoons dark molasses
2	teaspoons dry mustard
1	tablespoon Worcestershire sauce
1	teaspoon salt
1	cup beer

1. Drain the beans and transfer them to a large saucepan. Add water to cover them, add the bay leaf, and bring to a boil. Reduce the heat, cover, and simmer slowly for about 1 hour and 30 minutes or until tender.

2. Preheat the oven to 325°.

3. Drain the beans and reserve the cooking water. Discard the bay leaf. In a large mixing bowl combine the beans, onion, pork, molasses, and spices. Transfer the mixture to a bean pot or casserole dish with a tight-fitting lid.

4. In a saucepan bring the reserved water and beer to a boil. Pour over the beans until they are covered in the liquid. Bake tightly covered for 7 hours. Check the liquid level after about 5 hours. Add boiling water if needed to keep the water level above the beans.

5. Remove the lid, pull the pork slices to the top to brown, and bake uncovered for 1 hour.

Steamin' Swamp Stew

Serves 6

3	tablespoons all-purpose flour
½	teaspoon ground cumin
½	teaspoon chili powder
½	teaspoon ground cinnamon
1½	pounds chicken, boned, skinned, and cut into 1-inch cubes
2	tablespoons olive oil
1	tablespoon butter
4	cloves garlic, minced
1	cup low-sodium chicken stock
½	cup orange juice
6	small red potatoes, scrubbed and quartered
2	medium sweet potatoes, peeled and cubed
1	medium green bell pepper, seeded and cut into 2-inch strips
1	medium red bell pepper, seeded and cut into 2-inch strips
1	10-ounce can tomatoes with green chilies
1	8-ounce can tomato sauce
1	15-ounce can red kidney beans, drained
2	tablespoons drained capers
2	tablespoons chopped fresh cilantro
	Salt and freshly ground black pepper to taste
1	cup shredded Cheddar cheese

1. In a large mixing bowl combine the flour, cumin, chili powder, and cinnamon. Add the chicken and toss well to coat.

2. In a large heavy pot heat the olive oil and butter. Add the garlic and sauté for 1 minute. Add the chicken and sauté for 2 to 3 minutes. Add the chicken stock and

orange juice, bring to a boil briefly, then reduce the heat. Cover and simmer for 15 minutes.

3. Add the potatoes, sweet potatoes, bell peppers, tomatoes, tomato sauce, and kidney beans. Cover and simmer for 30 minutes or until the potatoes are tender.

4. Stir in the capers and chopped cilantro and season with salt and pepper. Serve in shallow bowls with shredded Cheddar on top.

Colonel Blake sends his regards.

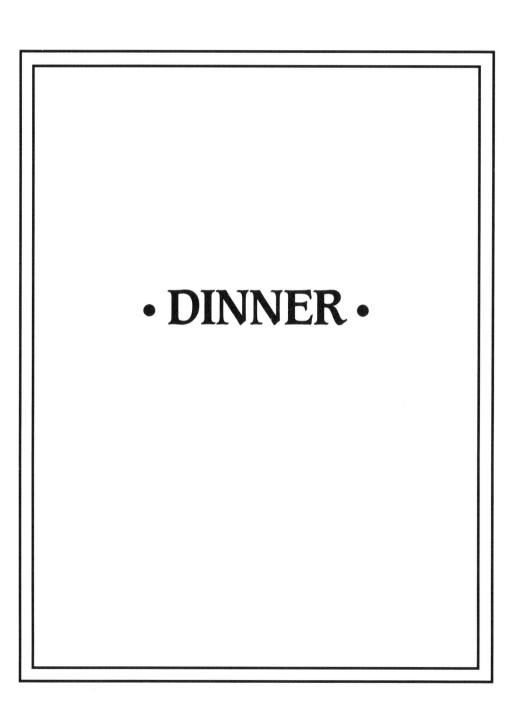

• DINNER •

OCEAN OF FISH

Brigadier Broiled Salmon

with Dijon Ranch Sauce

Serves 4

Cooking oil spray

1   1 ½-pound salmon fillet, skin removed

Salt and white pepper to taste

¼   cup white wine (or clam juice)

1   package original Ranch salad dressing mix

1   cup mayonnaise

1   cup buttermilk

¼   cup Dijon mustard

Parsley sprigs and lemon slices for garnish

1. Preheat the oven to 350°.

2. Generously spray a heavy ovenproof saucepan with oil and heat on high, just until the oil begins to smoke. Immediately add the salmon and sear for 2 minutes on each side. Remove from the heat, season with salt and pepper, and pour wine over the fish. Place the saucepan in the oven and bake the fish for 8 to 10 minutes.

3. While the fish is cooking, in a medium bowl combine the salad dressing mix, mayonnaise, buttermilk, and Dijon mustard and whisk until smooth. In a small saucepan heat 1 cup of the sauce over low-medium heat. Refrigerate the remaining sauce for another use.

3. Transfer the fish to a warm platter. Spoon the sauce over the salmon, garnish with parsley and lemon slices, and serve immediately.

Variation: Chicken or other fishes can be substituted with equally delicious results.

DINNER

Charles' Bahston Lobstah

with Bell Peppers Sautéed in Garlic Butter

Serves 4

1	head garlic
4	lobster tails, sliced lengthwise in half
¼	cup olive oil
6	tablespoons unsalted butter
1	large red bell pepper, seeded and diced
1	large yellow bell pepper, seeded and diced
1	large orange bell pepper, seeded and diced
	Salt and freshly ground black pepper to taste
3	tablespoons coarsely chopped fresh basil

1. Preheat the oven to 350°. Wrap the garlic head tightly in tin foil and bake for 1 hour.

2. When cool enough to handle, slice the top off the head to expose the inner cloves. Squeeze the garlic into a small bowl and set aside. Discard the garlic skin.

3. Preheat the barbecue grill to medium.

4. Brush the lobster meat with olive oil and grill for 6 to 8 minutes on each side. Be careful not to overcook.

5. In a large skillet melt the butter over medium-high heat. Mix in the roasted garlic and add the bell peppers, salt, and pepper. Sauté for 3 minutes, just until the peppers soften.

6. Place 2 lobster tail halves on each plate. Spoon peppers and garlic butter over each tail. Sprinkle with fresh basil and serve immediately.

DINNER

Orange Sniper Snapper

Serves 4

4	snapper fillets
¼	cup grated onion
2	tablespoons orange juice
2	tablespoons lemon juice
2	teaspoons grated orange peel (zest)
1	teaspoon grated nutmeg
1	medium lemon, thinly sliced

1. Preheat the oven to 350°.

2. Place the fish in a single layer, skin side down, in a baking dish. In a small bowl combine the onion, orange juice, lemon juice, and orange peel. Pour the mixture over the fish, cover and refrigerate for a minimum of 1 hour.

3. Sprinkle the fish with nutmeg then bake uncovered for 25 to 30 minutes. Garnish with lemon slices and serve.

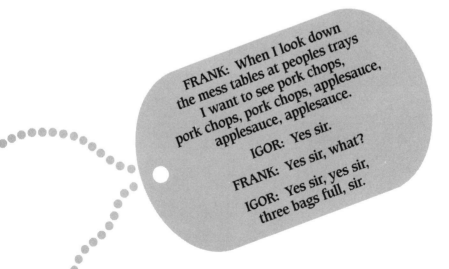

FRANK: When I look down the mess tables at peoples trays I want to see pork chops, pork chops, pork chops, applesauce, applesauce, applesauce.

IGOR: Yes sir.

FRANK: Yes sir, what?

IGOR: Yes sir, yes sir, three bags full, sir.

DINNER

Scalpel Scallops

with Spicy Tequila Cream Sauce

Serves 4

1	recipe Dress White Rice (see recipe, page 150)
2	tablespoons olive oil
¼	cup unsalted butter
3	cloves garlic, minced
1	pound sea scallops, sliced into thirds
2	ears fresh white or yellow corn, kernels cut from the cob
2	plum tomatoes, seeded and chopped
1	jalapeño pepper, minced
¼	cup tequila
⅛	cup heavy cream
1	lime, halved
½	teaspoon salt
½	teaspoon freshly ground black pepper

1. Prepare Dress White Rice, cover, and set aside.

2. In a large skillet heat the olive oil and butter over medium-high heat. Add the garlic and sauté for 1 minute. Add scallops and sauté for 2 minutes. Add the corn, tomatoes, and jalapeño pepper and sauté for 1 minute. Add the tequila and cream, and squeeze on the juice from the lime halves. Mix and bring to a boil. Allow to reduce slightly.

3. Transfer the rice to a warm platter. Pour the scallop mixture over the rice. Season with salt and pepper and serve immediately.

Variation: This dish is equally delicious served over cooked pasta.

Sparkey's Sockeye Salmon and Vegetable Hash

Serves 2 to 4

Cooking oil spray

1½ pounds salmon fillet, all skin removed

4 tablespoons butter or margarine

1 medium red bell pepper, diced

1 medium green bell pepper, diced

1 medium yellow bell pepper, diced

1 medium zucchini, diced

1 medium yam, peeled and diced

⅓ cup fresh lime juice (approx. 4 to 5 small limes)

Salt and pepper to taste

1. Preheat the oven to 350°.

2. Spray a large ovenproof nonstick skillet with cooking oil. Heat on high just until the oil begins to smoke. Sear the salmon fillet for 2 minutes on each side. Transfer the skillet to the oven and bake for 8 to 10 minutes.

3. In a large sauté pan melt 1 tablespoon of butter over medium-high heat. Add all of the vegetables and sauté for a few minutes until softened.

4. In a small saucepan melt 3 tablespoons of butter over medium-high heat. Stir constantly until the butter is golden brown. Remove from the heat and pour over the vegetables. Add the lime juice, salt, and pepper and bring to a simmer until heated through.

5. Transfer the salmon fillet to a serving platter. Pour the vegetable mixture over the fillet and serve.

Dear Ma,

Remember when I fell off Craig's horse, Sally, and busted my ribs? Colonel Potter told me that Sally might have stumbled because she got a rock stuck in her frog. Heck, I didn't know horses kept pets. Ha ha. Radar got the Colonel his own horse that he loves to ride around on whenever he can. One day he was brushing Sophie (that's the horses' name) and I asked him what was gonna happen to her when the war is over. His eyes got all misty, and he just smiled at her.

It's always nice serving his meals because he never makes me feel like it's my fault when the food isn't so good. Guess that's why he's a Colonel. I sure hope he gets a new horse when he gets home.

Love, Igor

Spearchucker's Shrimp

Serves 4

For the Sauce:

¼	cup olive oil
2	cloves garlic, chopped
2	yellow onions, thinly sliced
1	28-ounce can chopped tomatoes, undrained
¼	cup white wine
2	teaspoons dried oregano
¼	cup kalamata olives, pitted and coarsely chopped
	Salt and freshly ground black pepper to taste

1. In a large pot heat the olive oil over medium-low heat. Add the garlic and onions, and sauté until the onions are softened but not browned.

2. Add the tomatoes, wine, oregano, olives, salt, and pepper and mix thoroughly. Bring to a brief boil. Reduce the heat to low and simmer for 30 minutes or until the sauce is reduced by one-third. Remove from the heat, cover, and set aside.

For the Shrimp:

3	tablespoons unsalted butter
1½	tablespoons olive oil
4	large cloves garlic, chopped
1¼	pounds large shrimp, shelled and deveined
⅔	pound feta cheese, crumbled
1	recipe Dress White Rice (see recipe, page 150)
1	tablespoon chopped fresh parsley

DINNER

1. In a large skillet heat 2 tablespoons of butter and 1 tablespoon of olive oil over medium heat until hot. Add ½ of the chopped garlic and cook until lightly golden. Add just enough shrimp to cover the bottom of the skillet but not crowd. Cook until just opaque, turning once. Be careful not to overcook. Place the shrimp evenly in a 9 x 13-inch baking dish. Repeat the process with the remaining butter, oil, garlic, and shrimp.

2. Pour the tomato sauce over the shrimp then sprinkle on the feta cheese. At this point the dish may be held at room temperature for up to 1 hour if necessary.

3. Prepare the Dress White Rice. Mix in 1 tablespoon of unsalted butter and ½ tablespoon of olive oil to the cooked rice.

4. Preheat the broiler. Adjust the top rack to 6 inches from the broiler. Place the shrimp under the broiler for about 2 to 4 minutes or until the feta is golden brown.

5. Transfer the rice to a warm platter. Spoon the shrimp over the rice, sprinkle on chopped parsley, and serve immediately.

A couple of happy majors.

Stuffed Seoul

Serves 4

½	cup unsalted butter
1	cup chopped mushrooms
2	teaspoons garlic powder
1½	teaspoons basil
1	teaspoon onion powder
½	teaspoon salt or to taste
½	cup breadcrumbs
2	egg yolks
1	14-ounce can diced tomatoes
2	pounds sole fillets (12 equal size fillets)
½	cup vermouth
½	cup grated Parmesan cheese

1. Preheat the oven to 375°.

2. In a medium saucepan melt 1 tablespoon of butter over medium-high heat. Add the mushrooms and sauté for 1 minute.

3. Add the seasonings, breadcrumbs, egg yolks, and tomatoes and mix well.

4. Remove from the heat and spread the mixture evenly over each fillet. Roll up the fillets and secure with wooden picks.

5. Place the fillets seam-side down on a baking dish. Pour vermouth over the tops and sprinkle each with cheese. Dot the tops with butter and bake uncovered for 20 minutes. Remove the picks, transfer to a platter, and serve immediately.

It's not my fault that the food is lousy!

IGORISM:
You think that's brown, look at the mayonnaise.

Supply Clerk Scallops

Over Angel Hair Pasta with Pasilla Chili Sauce

Serves 4

For the Sauce:

3	pasilla chili peppers
1	8-ounce can tomatoes
3	cloves garlic, minced
¼	cup white wine
½	teaspoon ground cumin
½	teaspoon dry mustard
¼	teaspoon salt
½	teaspoon black pepper

Broil the chilies until the skins blacken and blister. Remove from the oven and let cool. When cool enough to handle, remove the skin and seeds. Chop coarsely, then place in a blender or food processor. Add the remaining ingredients and process until smooth. Reserve.

For the Pasta and Scallops:

½	teaspoon salt
1	pound angel hair pasta (capelli d'angelo)
2	tablespoons butter
2	cloves garlic, minced
1	pound bay scallops

1. In a large pot bring 4 quarts of water and ½ teaspoon salt to a boil. Cook the angel hair according to the package instructions.

DINNER

2. While the pasta is cooking, in a large heavy saucepan melt the butter over medium heat. Add the garlic and sauté for 1 minute. Add the pasilla sauce and scallops and simmer for 3 minutes.

3. Drain the cooked pasta well and transfer to a large bowl. Add the scallops and sauce and mix gently. Serve immediately.

Radar caught me 'n Sergeant Zale testin' some of the furniture.

DINNER

Three-Day-Pass Pasta

with Shrimp and Scallops

Serves 4

1	pound angel hair pasta (capelli d'angelo)
2	tablespoons unsalted butter
½	cup sliced mushrooms
3	fresh Roma tomatoes, chopped
1	tablespoon finely minced fresh garlic
1	tablespoon chopped fresh basil
	Salt and pepper to taste
¼	cup Marsala wine
1	cup prepared marinara sauce
½	cup half and half
¼	teaspoon Paul Prudhomme's Seafood Magic
1	teaspoon all-purpose flour
12	medium to large scallops
1½	tablespoons olive oil
16	medium shrimp, shelled and deveined

Note: The angel hair and shellfish are easy to overcook. Watch your time carefully with this dish.

1. In a large pot bring 4 quarts of water to a boil. Start cooking the angel hair according to the package instructions.

2. In a large heavy saucepan melt the butter over medium-high heat. Add the mushrooms, tomatoes, garlic, basil, salt, and pepper and sauté for 1½ minutes. Add the Marsala wine, marinara, half and half, Seafood Magic, and flour and bring to a boil. Reduce the heat, add the scallops, and simmer for 4 minutes.

3. Drain the cooked pasta well, then transfer to a large bowl. Add the olive oil and mix thoroughly. Cover to keep warm.

4. Add the shrimp to the sauce and cook for 2 minutes. Combine the sauce with the pasta and mix gently. Serve immediately.

Me and Klinger and Sergeant Zale messin' around with Radar.

FLAGG: They don't do two shows at the Sands on weekends.
HAWKEYE: How do you know that?
FLAGG: I was a showgirl there for six weeks.

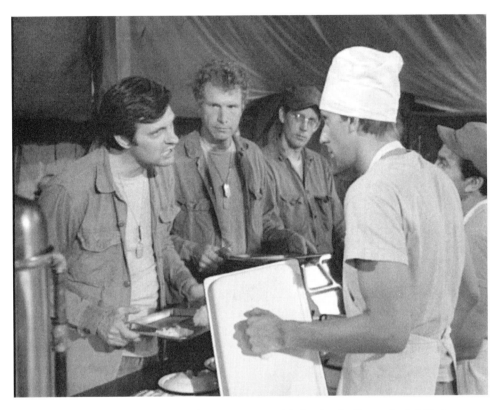

Here's Captain Pierce tellin' me he's not interested in havin' the liver. Who is? Ha ha.

"You Creamed The Vodka?"

Grilled Swordfish with Vodka Cream Sauce

Serves 4

¼	cup unsalted butter
1½	cups whipping cream
½	cup vodka
2	tablespoons green peppercorns, soaked in water, drained, and crushed
3	tablespoon fresh lime juice
¼	teaspoon salt
4	swordfish steaks (about 6 ounces each)
	Salt and freshly ground pepper to taste
1	fresh lime, quartered for garnish

1. Preheat the barbecue grill to medium-high.

2. In a medium saucepan melt the butter over medium heat. Add the cream and vodka and bring to a boil for about 4 minutes until slightly thickened. Stir in the peppercorns, lime juice, and salt. Cover, remove from heat, and set aside.

3. Season the swordfish with salt and pepper. Grill the steaks for 6 to 8 minutes or until the fish is opaque and flakes easily when tested with a fork. Turn once halfway through grilling time.

4. Transfer the steaks to individual plates. Spoon vodka cream sauce over each. Garnish with lime wedges and serve.

Potter's Pew-wy Pork Chops

Serves 4

For the Chops:

1	teaspoon onion powder
1	teaspoon garlic powder
½	teaspoon leaf thyme
½	teaspoon leaf oregano
½	teaspoon leaf basil
1	teaspoon salt
3	tablespoons paprika
1	teaspoon finely ground black pepper
½	teaspoon cayenne pepper
4	6-ounce pork chops

1. Combine all of the seasonings above and coat the chops with the mixture.

2. Heat an iron skillet until extremely hot. Cook the chops for about 4 to 5 minutes on each side, until blackened.

For the Sauce:

4	ounces Gorgonzola cheese, crumbled
4	ounces ricotta cheese
2	ounces grated Parmesan cheese
1	cup half and half

DINNER

1. In a medium saucepan combine the Gorgonzola, ricotta, Parmesan, and half and half. Stir constantly over low heat. Continue to heat until the sauce lightly bubbles.

2. Transfer the chops to individual plates, spoon the sauce over each chop, and serve.

Me and the Colonel enjoyin' a stogie.

Pork Choppers with Barbecue Sauce

Serves 4

For the Sauce:

Makes 2 cups

1	10½-ounce can tomato soup
¼	cup vinegar
⅓	cup firmly packed brown sugar
1	teaspoon nutmeg
1	teaspoon ground cinnamon
1	teaspoon ground allspice
1	teaspoon Worcestershire sauce

In a bowl combine all of the above ingredients. Can be made up to 3 days in advance and stored in the refrigerator.

For the Chops:

1	tablespoon vegetable oil
4	1½-inch (or thicker) pork chops
1	cup Barbecue Sauce (recipe above)

1. Preheat the oven to 350°.

2. In a heavy skillet heat the oil over high heat until extremely hot. Add the chops and sear them on both sides.

3. Transfer the chops to a baking pan and spoon on a liberal amount of Barbecue Sauce. Bake uncovered for 1 hour, adding sauce at 20 minute intervals.

Purple Heart Pork

Serves 4 to 6

1	boneless loin of pork (about 3½ pounds)
16	moist prunes, pitted and drained
	Salt and freshly ground black pepper
½	cup Madeira wine
½	cup water
1	tablespoon arrowroot mixed with ¼ cup water

1. Preheat the oven to 375°.

2. Make a pocket through the middle of the tenderloin with a long thin knife. Stuff the prunes into the pocket. Tie the pork with string to retain its shape and keep the pocket closed. Season with salt and pepper.

3. Place the pork in a shallow roasting pan, fat side up. Roast for two hours, turning every 15 minutes. Transfer to a heated platter and set aside.

4. Skim and discard the fat from the roasting pan. Mix the wine and water with the brown bits that remain in the pan. Bring the mixture to a boil and add the arrowroot mixture, stirring constantly until the gravy thickens. Season with salt and pepper to taste. Strain the gravy into a small mixing bowl and set aside.

5. Slice the pork and serve with the gravy.

Stun-Line Pork Chops

Marinated Pork Chops and Golden Garlic Grits

Serves 2

For the Pork Chops:

1	cup olive oil
1	tablespoon chopped fresh garlic
⅓	cup fresh lemon juice
1	teaspoon Cajun seasoning
4	pork chops, 1-inch thick or less

1. In a shallow dish combine the olive oil, garlic, lemon juice, and Cajun seasoning. Add the pork chops, cover, and marinate in the refrigerator for 24 hours.

2. Drain the pork chops. Heat a large, heavy skillet over high heat until extremely hot then add the pork chops. After searing, reduce the heat and cook the chops slowly until done, about 4 minutes on each side. The time depends on the thickness of the chop.

For the Grits:

1½	cups water
⅛	teaspoon salt
1	cup grits
4	ounces Velveeta cheese, cut into ½-inch cubes
4	dashes Tabasco sauce
½	teaspoon Worcestershire sauce
1	heaping teaspoon chopped fresh garlic

1. In a medium saucepan bring the water and salt to a boil. Slowly stir in the grits.

Cover, reduce the heat to low, and simmer for 5 minutes.

2. Add the remaining ingredients and stir until the cheese is thoroughly melted.

3. Divide the chops and grits onto individual plates and serve.

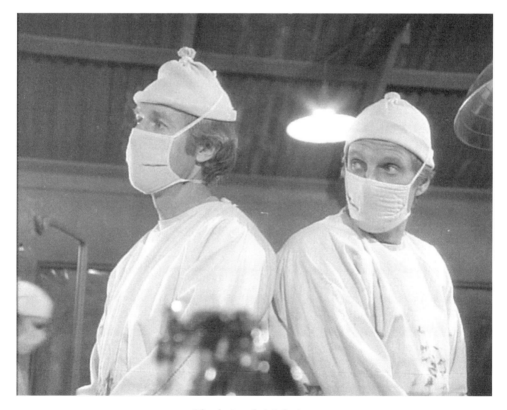

The doctors bein' doctors.

Dear Ma,

Remember when I boiled a banana and told Doug it was fruit stew? Funny, huh? Anyway, there's a surgeon here named B.J. Hunnicut (I wonder how many hunnies he cut—ha ha) who plays jokes all the time. One day he made Hawkeye crazy trying to figure out what joke was being played. The joke was, there was no joke. That was the joke. Get it? I didn't. When he first got here he shaved all the time. It didn't take long for him to grow a big mustache. I guess the Colonel lets him get away with it because he's a really good doctor. If little ol' me grew that much hair on my face you can bet I'd end up as Creamed Igor on a Shingle. Maybe I'll try it just as a joke. Ha ha.

          Love, Igor

IT'S BROWN—I HOPE IT'S MEAT

Adam's Ribs

Serves 2 to 3

3	pounds spareribs
1	lemon, sliced thinly
½	cup dry sherry
1	tablespoon brown sugar
2	tablespoons soy sauce
1	tablespoon sesame oil

1. Preheat the oven to 350°.

2. Cut the spareribs into serving pieces if the ribs are large and place on a rack in a roasting pan. Place the lemon slices over the meat and bake for 1 hour, turning the ribs once.

3. While the ribs are baking, in a small bowl combine the sherry, brown sugar, soy sauce, and sesame oil.

4. Pour out all of the fat from the pan. Remove the rack and return the ribs to the pan. Brush the ribs with the sauce and return the pan to the oven for 10 minutes. Turn the ribs and brush with the remaining sauce. Continue to cook for 10 more minutes or until brown.

DINNER

The Battle of Burgoo

Serves 12

4	pounds beef shanks
4	pounds chicken, cut into quarters
3	quarts chicken broth (or beef broth)
3	cups canned plum tomatoes (or 6 plum tomatoes, peeled, seeded, and chopped)
3	cups tomato purée
6	medium russet potatoes, quartered
6	carrots, peeled and thinly sliced
2	medium yellow onions, chopped
2	cups corn kernels
1½	cups shredded cabbage
1	cup sliced celery
1	cup thinly sliced okra
3	tablespoons Worcestershire sauce
1	tablespoon Tabasco sauce
1	teaspoon black pepper
½	teaspoon salt
2	cups frozen peas
1	cup chopped parsley

1. In a large heavy kettle combine the beef, chicken, and broth. Bring to a simmer and cook slowly until the meats are very tender and fall from the bones, about 2 hours and 30 minutes.

2. Remove the beef and chicken from the broth and chop into chunks. Discard the bones and return the meats to the broth.

3. Add all of the remaining ingredients except the peas and parsley. Simmer slowly, stirring occasionally, over low heat for about 2 hours or until the vegetables are soft and the stew is very thick.

4. Add the peas and parsley and cook for 10 minutes. Serve with crusty bread and additional Tabasco sauce on the side—for those who want MORE HEAT!

Oops, I don't know how I missed that tray. Ha ha.

DINNER

Gas Passer Chili

Serves 4 to 6

8	tablespoons olive oil, divided
1½	pounds chuck roast, coarsely ground
1½	pounds pork shoulder, cut into ½-inch cubes
6	cloves garlic, minced
2	large yellow onions, chopped
1	16-ounce can whole tomatoes, undrained
2	cups dark beer
1	8-ounce can prepared tomato sauce
5	serrano chilies, seeded and diced
1	cup chicken broth
½	cup chili powder
1	tablespoon ground cumin
1	tablespoon paprika
1	tablespoon salt
1	teaspoon chopped fresh oregano
1	teaspoon chopped fresh basil
10	dashes green Tabasco sauce
	Cayenne pepper to taste
3	tablespoons masa harina or cornmeal
4	tablespoons hot water

Note: A 16-ounce can of pinto or chili beans may be added for texture. In Texas, however, it is semi-legal to make a citizen's arrest on a cook using beans in their chili.

1. In a large heavy skillet heat 4 tablespoons of olive oil over medium-high heat. Add the meat and brown until there is no pink left. Remove from the heat, drain off the fat, and set aside.

2. In a large heavy pot heat 4 tablespoons of olive oil over medium heat. Add the garlic and onions and sauté for 5 minutes or until the onions are tender.

3. Add the browned meat and all of the remaining ingredients except the masa harina and hot water. Bring to a simmer, cover, and cook over low heat for 3 to 6 hours, stirring occasionally. More chicken broth may be added for a juicier version.

4. Mix the masa harina with hot water to make a light paste. Add to the chili 30 minutes before serving to thicken.

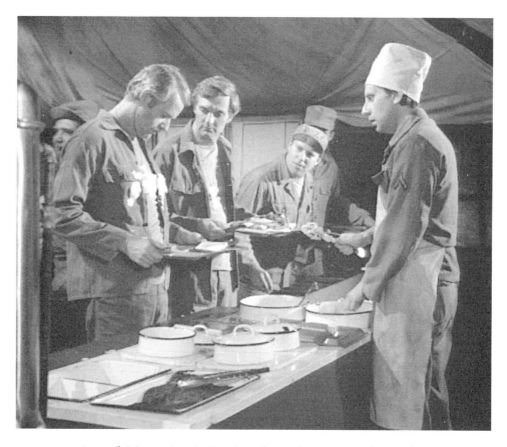

I'm explaining to Captain Hunnicutt that "Privates" can make mistakes.

Green Meat

Grilled Porterhouse Steaks with Tomatillo Sauce

Serves 4

For the Tomatillo Sauce:

Makes about 1 cup

¾	pound tomatillos, husks removed
2	jalapeño peppers, seeded and chopped
3	cloves garlic, chopped
½	cup chopped fresh cilantro
½	teaspoon ground cumin
½	teaspoon salt
½	teaspoon freshly ground black pepper
2	tablespoons fresh lime juice

1. Bring 2 quarts of salted water to a boil. Add the tomatillos and boil for 3 minutes. Drain and place under cold running water to stop cooking.

2. Transfer the tomatillos to a blender or food processor and add the remaining ingredients. Blend until smooth then set aside.

For the Steaks:

4	porterhouse or sirloin beef steaks, 1½ to 2 inches thick
	Salt and freshly ground black pepper to taste
2	cloves garlic, sliced in half
	Olive oil

1. Allow the steaks to stand at room temperature about 1 hour before cooking. Rub the steaks with cut garlic cloves.

2. Preheat the broiler or barbecue.

3. Grease the grill or grid with olive oil. Brown the meat on one side, then turn once and brown the other side. Allow about 8 minutes for each side for medium doneness.

4. Warm the Tomatillo Sauce over low heat just before serving. Transfer the steaks to individual plates and spoon sauce over each or serve on the side. Serve immediately.

Somebody slipped Captain Pierce a greasy rag for dinner.

DINNER

Hot Lips Tri-Tips

Serves 4

2	pounds beef tri-tips, trimmed of all fat
	Olive oil
	Salt and pepper to taste
⅛	teaspoon cayenne pepper
1	cup all-purpose flour
1	cup port wine
3	cups chicken broth
2	carrots, sliced
1	onion, sliced
4	celery stalks, chopped
2	garlic cloves, minced
1	serrano chili, seeded and minced
4	tablespoons butter
4	tablespoons flour
½	pound mushrooms, sliced

1. Preheat the oven to 450°. Brush the tri-tips with olive oil and season with salt, pepper, and cayenne. Dredge in flour.

2. In a large iron skillet brown the tri-tips over high heat.

3. Transfer to a roasting pan and add the wine, chicken broth, carrots, onion, celery, garlic, and chili. Cover and bake for 30 minutes. Reduce the oven temperature to 325° and bake for 45 minutes or until the internal temperature reaches 165°.

4. Transfer the tri-tips to a warm serving platter.

5. In a medium saucepan melt the butter over low heat, add the flour, and stir for 3 minutes to make a light roux. Add the juice and vegetables (from the roasting pan) and mushrooms and bring to a simmer for 1 minute, then pour the sauce over the tri-tips and serve.

Dear Ma,
Major Houlihan loves red meat. She comes back for seconds whenever we serve it. Radar says it makes her hot. I'm thinkin' of adding a lit-tle cayenne pepper to the meat and make it as hot as the Major! Ha, ha.
                    Love, Igor

DINNER

Meatball Surgery Meatballs

with Tomato Sauce

Serves 6

For the Meatballs:

Makes about twenty 2-inch balls

½	pound ground lamb
½	pound ground veal
½	pound ground pork
1	pound ground turkey
1	cup breadcrumbs
1	cup grated romano cheese
½	teaspoon salt
1	teaspoon pepper
3	eggs
3	tablespoons chopped parsley
3	cloves garlic, minced
1	cup plain tomato sauce
¼	cup water (if needed)
6	tablespoons olive oil

1. In a large mixing bowl combine the ground meats. Add the breadcrumbs, cheese, salt, and pepper and mix thoroughly.

2. In a blender combine the eggs, parsley, garlic, and tomato sauce and mix well. Add the mixture to the ground meat and blend thoroughly by hand to a semi-soft consistency. Add water if too dry.

3. Shape into 2-inch meatballs. In a large heavy skillet heat the olive oil over medium-high heat. Fry the meatballs until lightly browned. Remove from the heat and reserve.

For the Sauce:

¼   cup olive oil

3   cloves garlic, chopped

2   yellow onions, thinly sliced

2   28-ounce cans tomato purée

1   6-ounce can tomato paste

½   cup hearty red wine

3   tablespoons chopped fresh basil

     Salt and pepper

1½ pounds cooked pasta

1. In a large pot heat the olive oil over medium-low heat. Add the garlic and onions and sauté until the onions are softened but not browned.

2. Add the tomato purée, tomato paste, wine, basil, salt, and pepper and mix thoroughly.

3. Drop in the meatballs. Simmer on low, stirring occasionally, for 1 hour. Serve over cooked pasta.

HENRY: Holy Toledo, dog stew! Radar, these guys took your dog home in a people bag.

ROSIE: I'm sorry, Corporal.

RADAR: But they couldn't of. How could they eat a dog?

HENRY: Must have been a helluva bun.

DINNER

Mystery Meat Stew

Serves 6

2	pounds lean beef stew meat, cut into 1-inch cubes
4	large carrots, cut into 1-inch pieces
2	medium yellow onions, cut into 1-inch pieces
2	garlic cloves, minced
1	14½-ounce can tomatoes
1	8-ounce can tomato sauce
1½	cups beef broth
½	cup quick-cooking tapioca
1	teaspoon instant coffee granules
¼	teaspoon leaf thyme
½	teaspoon leaf oregano
½	teaspoon leaf basil
½	teaspoon salt

In a large ovenproof Dutch oven combine all of the ingredients. Cover and bake at 300° for 2 hours and 30 minutes to 3 hours, stirring every hour.

"I'm sure that was the same bacon that wrote Shakespeare's plays!"
—HAWKEYE

DINNER

The M*A*S*H Mess Casserole

Serves 10 to 12

8	ounces noodles or elbow macaroni
2	tablespoons olive oil
1	yellow onion, chopped
1	clove garlic, minced
2	pounds ground beef
1	8-ounce can tomato sauce
1	tablespoon Worcestershire sauce
1	tablespoon firmly packed brown sugar
2	teaspoons chili powder
2	teaspoons salt
¼	teaspoon pepper
1	4-ounce can mushroom pieces, undrained
1½	cups shredded Cheddar cheese

1. Preheat the oven to 350°.

2. Cook the noodles according to the package instructions.

3. While the pasta is cooking, heat the oil in a large skillet over medium-high heat. Add the onion and garlic and sauté for 2 to 3 minutes. Add the beef and sauté until all of the pink color disappears.

4. Drain the pasta well, transfer to a large mixing bowl and set aside.

5. To the beef add the tomato sauce, Worcestershire sauce, brown sugar, chili powder, salt, pepper, mushroom pieces, and 1 cup of Cheddar cheese and simmer for 5 minutes. Combine the mixture with the noodles then pour into a 3-quart casserole. Sprinkle with the remaining cheese and bake for 35 minutes.

DINNER

River of Liver

Breaded Dijon Calf's Liver with Herbs and Onions

Serves 6

6	slices calf's liver, sliced ½-inch thick, outside filament removed
	Salt and pepper
½	cup sifted all-purpose flour
7	tablespoons butter, divided
2	tablespoons vegetable oil, divided
3	tablespoons Dijon mustard
1	tablespoon minced shallots
3	tablespoons minced parsley
1	clove garlic, minced
3	cups fresh white breadcrumbs
6	yellow or white onions, thinly sliced

1. Season the liver with salt and pepper, then dredge the slices in flour. Heat 2 table-spoons butter and 1 tablespoon oil in a heavy skillet over medium-high heat. Sauté the liver for 1 minute on each side until just lightly browned. Transfer to a dish and set aside. Reserve the oil and butter.

2. In a medium mixing bowl combine the mustard, shallots, parsley, and garlic. Beat the mixture with a wire whisk or fork. Then add the reserved oil and butter slow-ly, while continuing to whisk until the mixture is creamy.

3. Coat the liver slices with the mustard sauce and then coat with breadcrumbs, cov-ering both sides. Shake off excess crumbs, then press the liver slices to adhere the crumbs to the liver. Can be prepared 3 to 4 hours in advance at this point. If so, cover and refrigerate. If not, place the liver on an oiled broiling pan and set aside.

4. In a large skillet heat 2 tablespoons of butter and 1 tablespoon of oil over medi-um-low heat until hot. Sauté the onions until lightly browned. Remove from the heat and cover to keep warm.

5. Preheat the broiler and adjust a rack to the top position.

6. Melt 3 tablespoons of butter. Baste the liver with half of the butter and broil for 1 to 2 minutes. Turn the liver, baste with the remaining butter, and quickly brown the other side. Transfer the liver to a warm platter, add the sautéed onions, and serve at once.

IGOR: Succotash, doc?

HAWKEYE: Yes, please.

IGOR: Potatoes?

HAWKEYE: Fine.

IGOR: Creamed corn?

HAWKEYE: Thank you.

IGOR: And for the entree today...

HAWKEYE: Here it comes.

TRAPPER: Steady.

IGOR: ...we have liver or fish.

HAWKEYE: I didn't hear you say that. Because it isn't possible. It's inhuman to serve the same food day after day. The Geneva Convention prohibits the killing of our taste buds.

TRAPPER: Easy.

HAWKEYE: I simply cannot eat the same food everyday. Fish. Liver. Day after day. I've eaten a river of liver and an ocean of fish. I've eaten so much fish, I'm ready to grow gills. I've eaten so much liver I can only make love if I'm smothered in bacon and onions. Are we gonna stand for this? We gonna let them do this to us? No, I say, no! We're not gonna eat this dreck any more! We want something else!

Captain Pierce couldn't wait to chomp into those ribs!

DINNER

Spam Lamb

Serves 4

2	pounds ground lamb
1	7-ounce can Spam, finely chopped
3	cloves garlic, minced
½	yellow onion, minced
1	tablespoon finely chopped fresh rosemary
	Salt and pepper to taste

1. Preheat the oven to 350°.

2. Combine the lamb and Spam in a large mixing bowl. Add the remaining ingredients and mix well.

3. Transfer the mixture to an ovenproof platter. Carefully form into the shape of a lamb and bake for 45 minutes.

Note: Visual impact of this dish may be enhanced by garnishing with a raw slice of yellow squash, a broccoli stalk and mushroom caps to represent the sun, a tree, and a mountain range.

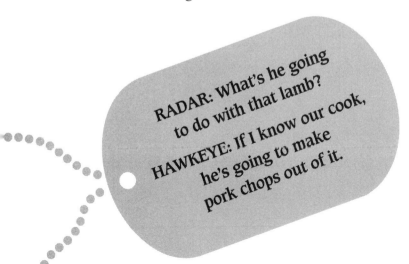

RADAR: What's he going to do with that lamb?

HAWKEYE: If I know our cook, he's going to make pork chops out of it.

FEELING FOWL

Chicken à la Igor

Serves 2

2	cups cooked chicken, cut into 1-inch cubes
1	cup heavy cream
2	tablespoons butter
2	tablespoons all-purpose flour
1	cup milk
	Salt and freshly ground white pepper
½	recipe M*A*S*H'd Potatoes with Roasted Garlic (see recipe, page 177)

1. In a heavy saucepan over low to medium heat add the chicken and cream and heat through. Remove from the heat and set aside.

2. In a small saucepan melt the butter and blend in the flour. Slowly stir in the milk until smooth to make a white sauce. Add the sauce to the chicken and bring to a simmer for 2 to 3 minutes. Add salt and pepper to taste.

3. Spoon the creamed chicken over M*A*S*H'd potatoes and serve immediately.

DINNER

This is the way Major Houlihan looks
when she's nursin' a patient. Yummy!

DINNER

Flaming Foxhole Chicken

Serves 3

1	tablespoon curry sauce
1	tablespoon oyster sauce
1	tablespoon sweet and sour sauce
½	teaspoon Chinese hot mustard
1	teaspoon water
½	teaspoon Chinese five spices
½	teaspoon cornstarch
½	teaspoon curry powder
½	teaspoon chili powder
½	teaspoon fish sauce
	Chili paste and sweet chili sauce to taste
3	large chicken breasts, boned and skinned
1	green bell pepper, diced
1	red bell pepper, diced
3	jalapeño peppers, minced
3	chili peppers, minced
½	bunch broccoli, chopped
4	mushrooms, sliced
1	cup Jasmine white rice
2	tablespoons sesame oil
2	cloves garlic, minced

1. In a small bowl, mix the curry, oyster, and sweet and sour sauces and Chinese mustard. Add the water, Chinese five spices, and cornstarch, blending thoroughly. Add the curry powder and ground chili powder, one at a time until mixed. Then add the fish sauce, chili paste, and sweet chili sauce. Mix thoroughly and set the sauce aside.

2. In a large mixing bowl combine the chicken, bell peppers, jalapeño, and chili peppers. Add the sauce and mix thoroughly.

3. Chop the broccoli and mushrooms and reserve.

4. Cook the rice according to the package instructions.

5. When the rice is almost done, preheat a wok or large skillet on high heat. The pan is ready when drops of water sprinkled into the pan evaporate on contact. Add the sesame oil and garlic. Quickly pour the chicken mixture into the wok, rapidly sautéing as you pour. Sauté the chicken until lightly browned then add the broccoli and mushrooms. Continue to sauté until the chicken is golden brown. Remove from the heat and cover.

6. Place a generous amount of rice in each of 3 bowls, making a well in the middle of the rice. Spoon the chicken mixture into the rice and serve.

Note: Always wash your hands thoroughly after working with hot peppers and any raw meat. The peppers can burn your eyes and the raw meat may contain dangerous bacteria.

KLINGER: Halt!
What's the password?

HAWKEYE: Outta my way
or I'll split your
head open.

KLINGER: Close enough.

I got this great watch from a guy named Minsoo. Sometimes it works.

"Radar, don't pick at your food. It'll never heal."
—HAWKEYE

DINNER

Gasmask Mustard Chicken

Serves 4

1	3½-pound chicken, cut into 8 pieces
	Salt and pepper to taste
1	teaspoon paprika
4	cloves garlic, minced
1	tablespoon Dijon mustard
½	cup dry white wine or vermouth
2	cups fresh breadcrumbs
¼	cup butter, melted
4	heads garlic, loose skin removed
2	tablespoons chopped fresh parsley

1. Preheat the oven to 350°.

2. Place the chicken pieces in a 9 x 13-inch baking pan. Season with salt, pepper, and paprika. Sprinkle on the chopped garlic.

3. In a small bowl combine the mustard and wine, then pour over the chicken. Sprinkle breadcrumbs over the chicken. Drizzle melted butter over the breadcrumbs. Place the garlic heads on top of the chicken.

4. Place in the top ⅓ of the oven and bake for 1 hour or until the chicken juices run clear and the top of the chicken is uniformly golden brown. Baste at 15 to 20 minute intervals while baking.

5. Transfer the chicken to a warm platter and sprinkle with chopped parsley. Serve 1 garlic head per person. Strain the pan juices into a bowl and serve on the side.

Serve with Creamy Green Potatoes (see recipe, page 172).

DINNER

Not The Colonel's Chicken

Chicken and Artichokes in Sherry

Serves 8

1	cup unsalted butter
1	pound mushrooms, sliced
4	pounds chicken pieces, breasts and legs
1	tablespoon salt
1	teaspoon pepper
2	9-ounce packages frozen artichoke hearts
1½	cups dry sherry
½	cup plus 3 tablespoons water
2	tablespoons cornstarch

1. In a large skillet melt ¼ cup of butter over medium-high heat. Add the mushrooms and sauté for about 3 minutes or until tender. Remove the skillet from the heat, transfer the mushrooms to a small bowl, and set aside.

2. Season the chicken pieces with salt and pepper. Return the skillet to medium-high heat and melt the remaining butter. Add the chicken and brown each piece on both sides.

3. Add the frozen artichoke hearts, sherry, ½ cup of water, and the mushrooms. Cover and simmer for 30 minutes.

4. Remove the chicken, artichokes, and mushrooms to a heated serving platter, then place in a warm oven. Stir the cornstarch and 3 tablespoons of water into a paste, and then blend into the juices that remain in the skillet. Cook, stirring occasionally, until the sauce thickens and boils.

5. Spoon the sauce over the chicken and vegetables and serve immediately.

Dear Ma,

The head guy here has three jobs – Commanding Officer, doctor, and Colonel. I think Colonel Blake is more doctor than Colonel though. Oh, he does all the Army stuff he's supposed to do, but he seems to like to get it out of the way and just have fun. At least as much fun as it's possible to have here.

Remember how funny Bill used to be? Well, the Colonel is even funnier! When he gets going, he cracks us all up. Everybody, except Major Burns, likes him a lot. You can tell he really cares about all the patients who end up here because he seems to worry about them.

We all just found out that he gets to go home. LUCKY GUY – sure wish I was gonna be on the plane with him!

Love, Igor

DINNER

Private Straminsky's Swollen Chicken

Serves 2

2	large pasilla chilies
3	large garlic cloves
2	large chicken breasts, boned and skinned
½	cup ricotta cheese
2	ounces feta cheese, crumbled
½	cup chopped fresh cilantro
½	small serrano chili, minced (or ⅛ teaspoon red pepper flakes)
1	tablespoon fresh lime juice
	Pepper to taste

1. Preheat the broiler. Roast the pasilla chilies on each side just until the skin blisters. Remove from the broiler and let cool. Roast the garlic cloves until golden brown. Remove from the broiler, let cool, then chop finely. Remove the stem and peel the skin from each chili, keeping the chili intact.

2. Preheat the barbecue grill to medium.

3. Pound the chicken breasts between wax paper to ¼-inch thickness and set aside.

4. In a small bowl combine the ricotta and feta cheeses. Add the cilantro, garlic, serano chili, lime juice, and pepper and mix thoroughly.

5. Cut an opening in the side of each of the roasted chilies. Carefully spoon the cheese mixture into the chilies, then close the openings. Place a stuffed chili on half of each pounded chicken breast, fold the chicken over it, and secure with toothpicks. It should look like a taco.

6. Barbecue 8 to 10 minutes on each side over low-medium heat. When the breasts are pierced with a fork the juices should run clear. Make sure there is no pink left in the meat.

Variation: After pounding the chicken breasts, marinate in your favorite recipe for 1 hour before barbecuing.

I took this picture with one hand and served with the other.

"Frank, you are ten of the most boring people I know."
—HAWKEYE

DINNER

Top Brass Pecan Chicken

with Madeira Wine Mushroom Sauce

Serves 4

½	cup finely chopped pecans
2	cups all-purpose flour
2	teaspoons Cajun seasoning
4	eggs, beaten
2	cups whole milk
¼	cup olive oil
4	chicken breasts, skinned and boned
1	cup chicken broth
⅔	cup Madeira wine
2	cups mushrooms, sliced
⅛	teaspoon salt
¼	teaspoon pepper
	Fresh parsley

1. Preheat the oven to 350°.

2. In a large mixing bowl combine the chopped pecans and flour. Add the Cajun seasoning, mixing well. In a separate bowl combine the eggs and milk. Dip each breast in the egg and milk mixture, then dredge through the flour mixture.

3. In a large sauté pan heat the olive oil over medium-high heat until the oil starts to smoke. Sauté the chicken breasts for 2 minutes on each side. Place the breasts in an ovenproof dish and bake for 5 minutes while the sauce is being cooked.

4. Discard the oil in the sauté pan and add the broth, wine, mushrooms, salt, and pepper. Bring to a boil. Blend 2 teaspoons of the flour mixture in 2 tablespoons of water. Stir into the sauce and cook for 2 minutes or until thickened.

5. Transfer the breasts to heated plates or a platter. Spoon the sauce over the breasts, top with chopped parsley, and garnish with parsley sprigs.

Winchester's Upper Crusted Chicken

Serves 4 to 6

1	3- to 3 ½-pound broiler-fryer chicken
2	tablespoons olive oil, divided
⅛	teaspoon cayenne pepper
¼	teaspoon salt
1	cup fresh breadcrumbs
¼	cup grated Parmesan cheese
¼	teaspoon leaf thyme
¼	teaspoon leaf basil
¼	teaspoon leaf oregano
⅛	teaspoon black pepper

1. Preheat the oven to 400°.

2. Cut the wing tips off of the chicken. Cut through the backbone and spread the chicken open. Lay bone side down, press flat, and pull the skin off. Place the chicken flesh-side up on a baking sheet sprayed with nonstick cooking oil spray.

3. In a small bowl mix 1 tablespoon of olive oil, cayenne pepper, and salt. Rub the mixture over the chicken and set aside.

4. Combine 1 tablespoon of olive oil with the breadcrumbs, Parmesan, thyme, basil, oregano, and pepper. Pat the mixture over the chicken. Bake for 30 to 35 minutes or until chicken is cooked through. Let cool 10 minutes before serving.

Father Mulcahy showin' off his garden.

Captain Hunnicut on a ride out of town.

PRIVATE PIZZA

Basic Training Pizza Dough

Makes one 14-inch pizza

1	package active dry yeast
¾	cup warm water (about 105°)
2	cups high gluten bread flour
½	teaspoon salt
	Olive oil

1. Dissolve the yeast in the water then pour it into a large mixing bowl. Pour the flour and salt on top and mix with a wooden spoon until it sticks together and comes away from the sides of the bowl. If it is too wet and sticky, add more flour. If too dry, add more water.

2. If mixing by hand, transfer the dough to a floured surface and knead it for 5 minutes into a ball. If using a food processor, combine the dissolved yeast, flour, and salt in a food processor fitted with a dough blade made of plastic. Be careful not to overmix. Mix only until a smooth dough ball is formed.

3. Lightly oil the dough ball, place in a glass bowl, and cover with plastic wrap. Let it rise for 1 hour or until doubled in size.

4. Place the dough on a floured surface and flour the dough liberally. Press the dough down by hand to let out the gasses. Roll with a rolling pin into a flat circle about ½-inch thick and 14-inches in diameter. Transfer to a lightly oiled pizza screen or a pan.

DINNER

Igor's Own Cheese Pizza

Serves 2

1	28-ounce can Italian style tomatoes
1	tablespoon olive oil
3	cloves garlic, chopped
½	6-ounce can tomato paste
1	heaping teaspoon dried basil
1	heaping teaspoon dried oregano
⅓	teaspoon cayenne pepper
½	teaspoon sugar
⅛	teaspoon salt
¼	teaspoon pepper
1	recipe Basic Training Pizza Dough (see recipe, page 145)
1	cup grated mozzarella cheese
1	cup grated imported Provolone cheese

1. Preheat the oven to 450°.

2. In a blender briefly chop the tomatoes coarsely. Reserve.

3. Heat the olive oil in a large skillet over medium-high heat. Add the garlic and sauté for 1 minute. Reduce the heat to low and add the tomatoes, tomato paste, and seasonings. Do not bring to a boil, stir until just heated through.

4. Ladle the sauce over the pizza dough. Then sprinkle on the cheeses and bake for 10 to 15 minutes.

DINNER

Victorious Veggie Pizza Pie

Serves 2

4	fresh artichokes
1	large red bell pepper
2	cups fresh button mushrooms
¼	cup extra-virgin olive oil
3	cups tomato paste
1	recipe Basic Training Pizza Dough (see recipe, page 145)
1	pound Jarlsberg cheese, grated
1½	teaspoons fresh oregano

1. Boil the artichokes for about 40 minutes. Let cool, then remove the stems and leaves until only the hearts remain. Chop the hearts into bite-sized pieces and set aside.

2. Roast the bell pepper under a broiler until the skin has blackened and blistered. Let cool for about 10 minutes. Skin and seed the pepper, then slice into strips and set aside.

3. Lightly coat a skillet with olive oil and sauté the mushrooms over medium-high heat, just until their moisture is released. Remove from the heat and set aside.

4. Preheat the oven to 450°.

5. In a medium bowl, combine the olive oil and tomato paste so that it's easy to spread on the dough, like an acrylic paint. (It's not really a sauce, it's an acrylic spread.)

6. Spoon on and spread a thin layer of tomato paste over the pizza dough up to about ½-inch from the edges. Remember, it's not a sauce per se and doesn't spread easily, so take care not to tear the dough. Sprinkle the Jarlsberg over the sauce. Next place the artichoke hearts on top of the cheese. Then add the mushrooms and peppers.

7. Bake for about 12 minutes. Remove from the oven, sprinkle on fresh oregano, and serve.

DINNER

I don't want to worry you but there is a war goin' on over here.
The doctors got away unharmed.

Dennis and Roy, a couple of my buddies, are solving a problem.

KOREAN GARLIC ATTACK

Blazin' Bulgogi

Korean Grilled Beef

Serves 4

1	pound thinly sliced beef
10	cloves garlic, finely minced
½	cup low-sodium soy sauce
½	cup sesame oil
2	teaspoons black pepper
½	cup green onions, quarter the white section lengthwise, then cut the whole onion into 1-inch pieces

1. Preheat the barbecue grill to high.

2. In a large mixing bowl separate the beef slices. Add the garlic, soy sauce, sesame oil, and pepper, and mix thoroughly. Add the green onion. Gently mix by hand while massaging the meat.

3. On a closely spaced grid, grill the meat, tossing constantly, until cooked through, about 3 to 5 minutes.

4. Transfer to a large bowl and serve with rice and chopsticks.

Variation: This dish is also excellent using chicken in place of the beef.

Dress White Rice

Serves 6 to 8

2   **cups white rice**

3   **cups water**

1. Pour the rice into a large heavy saucepan and add water to ¾ full. Stir the rice with your hand until the water is cloudy. Pour off the cloudy water and repeat this process until the rinse water is clear.

2. Add 3 cups of water to the drained rice and bring to a boil. Cover, reduce the heat, and simmer for 20 minutes or until all of the water is absorbed.

    Note: It is normal for the rice at the bottom to stick a little and brown lightly.

This is Minsoo's house, where I learned how to make Korean food.

Dear Ma,

Yo bo se yo – that means hello in Korean. The Korean people I've met here are really nice. Some of them live right outside the camp in little houses we call hooches. They make our house look like a mansion, but they're neat once you get used to dirt for a floor. I kinda like it – ha ha. Anyway, I got to know this guy, Minsoo, who is always outside the base selling neat stuff. He speaks pretty good English, and really loves American cigars and Celia, one of our nurses. She just got shipped home (lucky!) but Minsoo says he's gonna come to America, find Celia and marry her, even if it takes him ten years to do it! The thing is, he invited me to have dinner with his family for a real Korean meal. Ma, this food was so delicious I made sure to write down everything he did. If you try these recipes, please invite Janine over. There's so much garlic in the food that the jerk she works for won't ever try to kiss her again. Ha ha.

          Love, Igor

DINNER

Infirmary Eggplant

Serves 4

2   medium Japanese eggplants, cut lengthwise into ¼-inch slices

1   tablespoon rice vinegar

     Salt and pepper to taste

     Sesame seeds for garnish

1. Place the eggplant slices in a steamer and steam for 3 minutes or until soft.

2. Transfer the eggplant to a bowl and mix with vinegar, salt, and pepper. Transfer to a serving dish, sprinkle with sesame seeds, and serve.

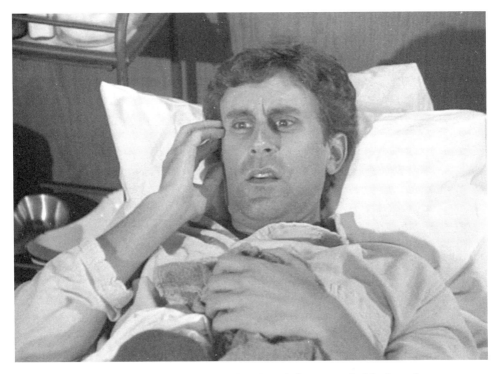

Don't look that bad, but I was sick, sick, sick from some foul fowl. Ha ha.

DINNER

Kim Chi

2	Napa cabbages, outer layers and core removed, washed and coarsely chopped
½	cup coarse salt
1	quart water
1	tablespoon red pepper flakes
6	cloves garlic, minced
2	tablespoons grated fresh ginger
1	tablespoon sugar
2	green onions, finely chopped

1. Place the cabbage in a large bowl. Sprinkle with salt, add water, and let stand for 15 minutes.

2. Rinse the cabbage in cold water and drain. Combine with the remaining ingredients and mix well.

3. Divide into quart jars, cover, and refrigerate. Allow to ripen for at least 4 to 5 days.

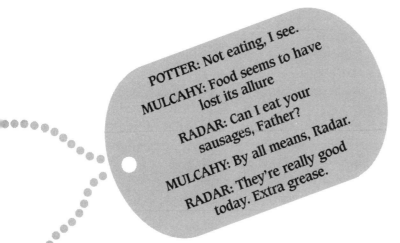

POTTER: Not eating, I see.
MULCAHY: Food seems to have lost its allure
RADAR: Can I eat your sausages, Father?
MULCAHY: By all means, Radar.
RADAR: They're really good today. Extra grease.

Korean Bean Sprouts

Pahn Chan

Serves 4 to 6

2	tablespoons sesame oil
2	cloves garlic, minced
2	cups Korean bean sprouts (rather large, found in Korean markets), rinsed, stems removed
1	tablespoon rice vinegar
	Pepper to taste
1	green onion, finely chopped

1. In a large wok or sauté pan over high heat add the oil and garlic. Very quickly add the bean sprouts and stir fry briefly.

2. Transfer immediately to a bowl and toss with rice vinegar and pepper. Sprinkle green onion on top and serve.

"Our steward of the stewpot? That beady-eyed simpleton is writing about gourmet cooking? Lucretia Borgia knows more. An unsuspecting reader might get the impression that Igor's recipes could somehow lead to food."
—CHARLES

DINNER

Local Yokel Korean Squash

Serves 2

1   teaspoon sesame oil

2   medium zucchini, cut into 1-inch cubes

2   cloves garlic, minced

2   tablespoons soy sauce

    Pepper to taste

1. In a medium skillet heat the sesame oil over high heat. Add the zucchini, garlic, soy sauce, and pepper and sauté for 2 minutes until tender.

2. Cover and continue to cook on high heat for 1½ minutes. Transfer to a small bowl and serve.

Variation: Korean Tofu. This same dish can be prepared using 1 package of firm tofu, cut into 1 x 2-inch cubes.

DINNER

Off Base Korean Warm Salad

Jap Chae

Serves 6 to 8

½   cup sesame oil

3   cloves garlic, politely minced

1½   cups snow peas

3   green onions, quarter the white section lengthwise, then cut the entire onion into 1-inch long pieces

1   cup enoki mushrooms

1½   cups dried black mushrooms, soaked in warm water for about 30 minutes or until soft and spongy

1½   cups dried shiitake mushrooms, stems removed, soaked in warm water for 30 minutes or until soft and spongy

1   yellow onion, halved then julienned

1½   cups carrots, julienned into 2-inch lengths

1   cup Korean leeks, poached briefly then cut into 1" length pieces
      Black pepper to taste

4   cups dried Korean vermicelli or glass noodles (spaghetti-like in thickness), soaked in warm water for 30 minutes

⅓   cup low-sodium soy sauce

1. In a large skillet heat the sesame oil over high heat. Add all of the vegetables and pepper and sauté for 2 minutes.

2. Add the noodles and soy sauce, stirring constantly, and cook for 3 minutes.

3. Transfer to a large serving bowl and let stand for a few minutes. Serve warm.

Variation: Any type of cooked meat or shellfish can be added to this dish.

Note: All Korean dishes are made with bite-size portions. There are no courses per se. Many dishes are usually served all together at one time.

DINNER

Rosey's Red Chili Pork

Dae Jigogi

Serves 4

1	pound thinly sliced pork butt
5	tablespoons hot bean paste (red chili paste, found at Korean markets)
½	cup sesame oil
4	cloves garlic, finely minced
	Salt and pepper to taste

1. Preheat the barbecue grill to high.

2. In a large mixing bowl separate the pork slices. Add all of the ingredients and mix thoroughly.

3. On a closely spaced grid, grill the meat, tossing constantly, until cooked through, about 3 to 5 minutes.

4. Transfer to a large bowl and serve with rice and chopsticks.

"You should have been in the Army before they taught chickens to lay powdered eggs. In World War I, I ate turnips for breakfast every day for a week. My tongue smelled like Arthur Murray's foot bath."
—COLONEL POTTER

DINNER

Steamtable Spinach

Serves 4

1	bunch fresh spinach, rinsed well
1	clove garlic, finely minced
1	tablespoon sesame oil
	Freshly ground pepper to taste

1. Steam the spinach until just limp. Rinse with cool water and let drain until the spinach is cool enough to handle.

2. Squeeze all of the water out of the spinach and place in a large mixing bowl. Add the remaining ingredients, mix, and serve.

Captain Hunnicutt wouldn't even try the creamed turnips.

M*A*S*H MACARONI

Fractured Fusilli

with Balsamic-Pepper Sauce

Serves 4 to 6 as a first course

1	tablespoon olive oil
2	cloves garlic, chopped
3	large red bell peppers, chopped
1	pound fusilli pasta
1	tablespoon olive oil
¼	cup balsamic vinegar
1	teaspoon leaf basil
1	teaspoon leaf oregano
¼	teaspoon salt
⅛	teaspoon cayenne pepper

1. In a medium stock pot heat 1 tablespoon of olive oil and the garlic over low heat. Add the red peppers and cook for 30 minutes, stirring frequently.

2. While the peppers are cooking, prepare the pasta according to the package instructions. Drain well and transfer to a large serving bowl. Add 1 tablespoon of olive oil and mix thoroughly. Cover to keep warm.

3. Transfer the peppers to the bowl of a food processor fitted with the steel blade. Add the remaining ingredients. Process until smooth, scraping the sides frequently with a rubber spatula. Transfer the pepper sauce back into the pot and heat through.

4. Add the sauce to the pasta, mix thoroughly, and serve immediately.

Dear Ma,

Pork sausage, pork sausage, pork sausage. Ma, call me nuts, but didn't any-body think of stuffing a sausage with a different critter! Remember how Uncle Grant used to smoke his ducks and turkeys? So, what if you put them (not all at one time—ha ha) in a sausage. And, instead of just salt and pepper, what if you seasoned them with fresh herbs and stuff. The Army won't let me try anything like that here, but I'll write you some ideas of my own and you can test 'em on Pop and everybody back home. You know, I gotta do it "by the book!"

Captain Pierce told Captain Burns that he should be stuffed in a sausage. Prob'ly be chewier than the pork. Ha ha.

Love, Igor

DINNER

Hawkeye and Trapper's Swamp Spaghetti

Fettucine with Shrimp, Red Bell Peppers, and Pine Nuts

Serves 4

½   pound plain fettucine

½   pound Cajun fettucine (or other spicy pasta)

4   tablespoons olive oil, divided

2   medium red bell peppers, cut lengthwise into ¼-inch slices

2   tablespoons finely minced fresh garlic

½   cup pine nuts, toasted (toast 10 minutes at 350°)

    Salt and pepper to taste

½   cup clam juice

24   large shrimp, shelled and deveined

2   tablespoons fresh basil, chopped

½   cup grated Parmesan cheese

    Fresh lemon slices for garnish

    Fresh basil sprigs for garnish

1. In a large pot, bring 4 quarts of water to a boil. Cook the fettucine according to the package instructions. Drain well and transfer to a mixing bowl. Add 2 tablespoons of olive oil and mix thoroughly. Cover to keep warm.

2. In a large saucepan heat 2 tablespoons of olive oil over medium-high heat. Add the red bell pepper and sauté for 1 minute. Add the garlic, pine nuts, salt, and pepper and sauté for 1 minute.

3. Add the clam juice and bring to a boil. Add the shrimp and basil and sauté for 2 minutes, then turn the shrimp and sauté for 1 minute.

4. Add the shrimp mixture to the pasta, mixing thoroughly. Transfer to individual pasta bowls and top each with grated Parmesan cheese. Garnish with a lemon slice and a sprig of fresh basil.

DINNER

Rat-A-Tat Touille

Serves 4

1	pound penne pasta
3	tablespoons olive oil, divided
2	tablespoons garlic, chopped
1	red bell pepper, cut lengthwise in ¼-inch strips
1	green bell pepper, cut lengthwise in ¼-inch strips
1	large yellow onion, quartered and separated
½	eggplant, peeled, cut lengthwise into ½-inch slices and soaked in cool water for 30 minutes, then cubed
1	medium-large zucchini, cut into ½-inch slices
2	yellow crookneck squash, cut into ½-inch slices
3	plum tomatoes, cored, quartered, seeded and cut into ½-inch strips
1	cup medium mushrooms, halved
1	cup chicken broth
1	tablespoon chopped fresh basil
⅛	teaspoon leaf oregano
	Salt and pepper to taste
½	cup Marsala wine
1	cup prepared marinara sauce
	Fresh basil sprigs for garnish

1. Cook the penne according to the package instructions and drain well. Transfer to a large mixing bowl and add 1 tablespoon olive oil and mix thoroughly. Cover to keep warm.

2. In a large sauté pan heat 2 tablespoons of olive oil over medium-high heat. Add the garlic, red and green bell peppers, and onion and sauté for 2 minutes until the peppers have softened. Add the eggplant, zucchini, squash, tomatoes, mushrooms, chicken broth, basil, oregano, salt, and pepper and cook for 2 minutes. Add the Marsala and marinara and cook for 2 to 3 minutes.

3. Combine the mixture with the pasta and mix thoroughly. Transfer to a large platter or individual plates and garnish with fresh basil sprigs.

It wasn't easy findin' a bathtub in Korea.

Rapid Fire Fusilli

with Grilled Chicken, Artichoke Hearts, and Sun-dried Tomatoes

Serves 4

2	cups dry white wine
2	tablespoons lemon juice
3	cloves garlic, finely minced
⅛	teaspoon salt
¼	teaspoon pepper
4	boneless chicken breasts, skin removed
1	pound fusilli pasta
3	tablespoons olive oil, divided
2	teaspoons chopped fresh garlic
⅔	cup chicken broth
½	cup dry sherry
½	cup sun-dried tomatoes, soaked in hot water for 5 minutes, then julienned
6	artichoke hearts, drained and quartered
¼	cup toasted pine nuts (toast for 10 minutes at 350°)
2	tablespoons chopped fresh basil
⅛	teaspooon salt
¼	teaspoon pepper
⅔	cup grated Parmesan cheese

1. In a shallow bowl combine the wine, lemon juice, and seasonings. Add the chicken, cover, and marinate in the refrigerator for at least 1 hour.

2. Preheat the barbecue grill. In a large pot for the pasta, bring 4 quarts of water to a boil.

3. Cook the fusilli according to the package instructions. Drain well and transfer to a mixing bowl. Add 2 tablespoons of olive oil and mix thoroughly. Cover to keep warm.

4. Grill the chicken breasts for 20 to 30 minutes on each side or until the juices run clear. Remove from the grill. Slice the chicken breasts into ½-inch wide strips.

5. Heat 1 tablespoon of olive oil and the garlic in a large sauté pan over medium heat. Add the chicken broth, sherry wine, and tomatoes and cook for 2 minutes. Then add the chicken, artichoke hearts, pine nuts, basil, salt, and pepper and cook for 2 minutes, until the chicken is thoroughly heated through. Add the grated Parmesan cheese, then combine the mixture with the pasta, tossing until the fusilli is coated.

6. Divide the fusilli among individual pasta bowls. Arrange the grilled chicken like spokes in a wheel. Garnish with a slice of lemon.

Here's me tellin' a great joke.

Rizzo's Motor Pool Penne

with Cajun Garlic Shrimp

Serves 4

1	pound penne pasta
2	tablespoons olive oil, divided
1	tablespoon unsalted butter
1	tablespoon chopped fresh garlic
½	teaspoon crushed red pepper flakes
2	tablespoons chopped fresh basil
2	tablespoons chopped green onions
2	teaspoons Worcestershire sauce
½	teaspoon shrimp base (if available)
¼	cup Chablis
¼	cup dry sherry
2	tablespoons fresh lemon juice
1½	cups clam juice
	Salt and pepper to taste
24	large uncooked shrimp, shelled and deveined

1. In a large pot cook the penne according to the package instructions. Drain well and transfer to a large serving bowl. Add 1 tablespoon of olive oil and mix thoroughly. Cover to keep warm.

2. In a large sauté pan heat the butter and remaining olive oil over medium heat until the butter is bubbly and hot. Add the garlic, crushed pepper flakes, basil, and green onions and cook for 1 minute.

3. Add the Worcestershire sauce, shrimp base, Chablis, dry sherry, lemon juice and clam juice and bring to a boil. Add the shrimp, reduce the heat slightly and cook for 2 minutes on each side. Add salt and pepper

4. Combine the shrimp mixture with the pasta and mix thoroughly. Garnish with a sprig of basil and a couple of lemon slices.

DINNER

Here's the Colonel and Klinger and a visitor enjoyin' my joke.

Tellin' that joke knocked me out!

Sergeant Bustyer Gutt's Lasagna

Serves 8 to 10

4	ounces bacon (about 4 slices), cut into 1-inch pieces
1	medium yellow onion, chopped
2	cups sliced mushrooms
8	cloves garlic, finely minced
1	cup hearty red wine
4	tablespoons safflower or corn oil
1	pound lean ground beef
1	14-ounce can beef broth
1	pound lasagna noodles (approximately 15 pieces)
1	35-ounce can puréed tomatoes
1	6-ounce can tomato paste
1	cup water
1	teaspoon leaf oregano
1	teaspoon leaf basil
3	bay leaves
	Salt and pepper to taste
4	dashes Tabasco sauce
1	15-ounce container ricotta cheese
4	cups grated mozzarella cheese
1	cup grated Parmesan cheese

1. In a heavy skillet cook the bacon over medium-high heat until crisp. Remove the bacon, leaving the fat in the pan (use the bacon in another recipe). Add the onion and sauté over medium-high heat for 5 minutes, stirring frequently. Add the mushrooms and sauté for 8 minutes, stirring frequently. Add the garlic and sauté for 2 minutes. The onions should be golden brown and the mushrooms should be lightly crispy. Add the wine to the mixture and transfer it to a large, heavy saucepan.

DINNER

2. In a heavy pan heat the oil over high heat. Brown the meat (about 8 minutes), stirring often to break up any lumps . Drain the meat and transfer into the pot with the onions and mushroom mixture. Add the beef broth.

3. Preheat the oven to 350°. Butter a 9 x 13-inch baking dish.

4. Cook the pasta according to the package instructions. Be sure not to overcook. Drain it well and when cool enough to handle, lay each piece on wax paper to prevent them from sticking together and allow to dry.

5. Bring the beef mixture to a boil and reduce the liquid by two-thirds. Add the tomato purée, tomato paste, water, oregano, basil, bay leaves, salt, pepper, and Tabasco and return the sauce to a boil. Reduce the heat and simmer for 30 minutes, stirring often.

6. Cover the bottom of the baking dish with one layer of noodles. Spread one-third of the ricotta cheese over the pasta layer, then spread 1½ cups of meat sauce over the cheese, then sprinkle one-third of the grated mozzarella then one-third of the grated Parmesan over the sauce.

7. Repeat with another layer of pasta, ricotta cheese, meat sauce, mozzarella, and Parmesan cheese. Finally make a third layer in the same order.

8. Bake for 40 to 45 minutes until cheese is melted and lightly browned. Let it rest for 15 minutes before serving. This dish is best prepared a day in advance. If you do, cover with aluminum foil and refrigerate, then reheat it covered in a preheated 350° oven for 30 minutes or until heated through.

"I believe that marriage is the headstone of society."
—FRANK

DINNER

That's Major Winchester doin' some early morning paperwork in the mess tent. It was really hot that morning—that's me sweatin'.

Here I am trying to cool Major Winchester off. It's not workin'

DINNER

Winchester's Wilted Lettuce

Chicken Caesar Salad Pasta

Serves 2 to 4

1	cup Bread Bullets (see recipe, page 53) or prepared seasoned croutons
6	cloves garlic, chopped
1	2-ounce tin anchovy fillets
1	pound fusilli pasta
½	cup extra-virgin olive oil, divided
1	pound chicken breasts, skinned, boned, and cut into 1 x 2-inch pieces
2	cups chopped romaine lettuce
2	tablespoons lemon pepper
½	cup grated Parmesan cheese
½	cup pine nuts, toasted (toast 10 minutes at 350°)

1. In a blender or food processor fitted with the steel blade process the croutons into crumbs. Transfer to a bowl and reserve. Add the anchovy fillets and garlic to the processor and mix until smooth. Transfer to a small dish and reserve.

2. In a large pot bring 4 quarts of water to a boil. Cook the fusilli according to the package instructions. Drain well and transfer to a large serving bowl. Add 2 tablespoons of olive oil and mix thoroughly. Cover to keep warm.

3. In a large skillet heat the remaining olive oil over medium heat. Add the garlic and anchovy mixture and sauté for 1 minute. Add the chicken and sauté for 2 to 3 minutes or until the chicken is opaque on all sides. Add the romaine and sauté until the lettuce begins to wilt. Mix in the crouton crumbs and lemon pepper, then immediately add the mixture to the cooked fusilli. Add the Parmesan and pine nuts, mix well, and serve.

POTENT POTATOES

Creamy Green Potatoes

Mashed Potatoes with Pesto

Serves 6

½   teaspoon salt

2   pounds russet potatoes, (about 6 medium) peeled and quartered

1   cup fresh basil, loosely packed

3   cloves garlic, minced

¼   cup olive oil

3   tablespoons grated Parmesan cheese

¼   cup sour cream

¼   cup butter, melted

¼   cup milk

Salt and pepper to taste

1. In a large pot bring 4 quarts of water and ½ teaspoon of salt to a boil. Add the potatoes and cook covered for 20 to 40 minutes until tender.

2. While the potatoes are cooking, combine the basil, garlic, olive oil, and Parmesan cheese in the bowl of a food processor fitted with the steel blade. Process until smooth. Set the pesto aside.

3. Transfer the potatoes to a large mixing bowl and mash with a potato masher or fork. Add the sour cream, butter, milk, salt, and pepper, and beat with an electric mixer until smooth.

4. Add the pesto and mix well. Serve immediately.

Captain Pierce cracks us up with a funny PA announcement.

KLINGER: How can you eat this slop?
RADAR: My taste buds are tone deaf.

DINNER

Dud Spuds

Serves 6 to 8

3	tablespoons unsalted butter
1	clove garlic, minced
½	cup thinly sliced carrots
½	celery rib, diced
11	large yellow onions, thinly sliced
4	cups russet potatoes, diced
2	cups chicken stock
1½	teaspoons salt
¼	teaspoon pepper
1	teaspoon parsley flakes
2	cups milk
½	cup grated Cheddar cheese

1. In a large saucepan melt the butter over medium-high heat. Add the garlic, carrots, celery, and onions and sauté until the onions are soft and clear.

2. Add the potatoes, chicken stock, salt, pepper, and parsley and bring to a boil. Reduce the heat, cover, and simmer slowly for about 8 to 10 minutes until the potatoes are tender, stirring occasionally.

3. Stir in the milk and heat, but do not bring to a boil. Transfer to a large serving bowl and garnish with grated Cheddar cheese. Serve.

DINNER

Hot Potato Pucks!

Serves 4

4	russet potatoes, peeled and grated
1	yellow onion, grated
2	eggs, beaten
2	tablespoons matzo meal
½	teaspoon salt
½	teaspoon pepper
	Vegetable oil for frying
	Sour cream or applesauce

1. Place the potato and onion gratings in a muslin towel and wring to squeeze out as much moisture as possible. Transfer to a bowl and combine with the eggs, matzo meal, salt, and pepper.

2. In a heavy skillet heat ½-inch or more of oil over medium-high heat. Drop about 1 tablespoon of potato mixture in the skillet, forming patties, and fry until browned. Turn and brown the other side until crisp.

3. Drain on paper towels. To hold until all the batter is cooked, place them in a 200° oven. Serve with sour cream or applesauce.

"Our food here leaves a lot to be desired. Oh, it fills you up if you can keep it down."
—COLONEL BLAKE

DINNER

Potato Bacon Blitz

Mashed Potatoes with Bacon and Roasted Peppers

Serves 6

½   teaspoon salt

2   pounds russet potatoes, (about 6 medium) peeled and quartered

¼   cup unsalted butter

½   cup heavy cream, warmed over low heat

3   slices bacon, cooked and crumbled

3   cloves garlic, minced

1   7-ounce jar roasted red peppers, drained and chopped

     Salt and pepper to taste

1. In a large pot bring 4 quarts of water and ½ teaspoon of salt to a boil. Add the potatoes and cook covered for 20 to 40 minutes until tender. Drain.

2. Transfer the potatoes to a large mixing bowl and mash with a potato masher or fork. Add the butter and cream and beat with a fork until creamy.

3. Add the crumbled bacon, garlic, red peppers, salt, and pepper and mix well. Serve immediately, or keep the potatoes warm by placing the bowl in a large pan of hot water.

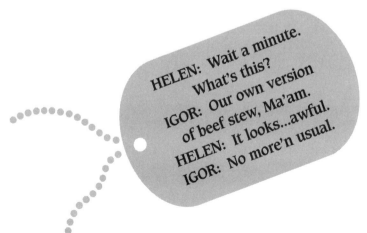

HELEN: Wait a minute. What's this?

IGOR: Our own version of beef stew, Ma'am.

HELEN: It looks...awful.

IGOR: No more'n usual.

M*A*S*H'd Potatoes with Roasted Garlic

Serves 6

1   medium head garlic

½   teaspoon salt

2   pounds russet potatoes (about 6 medium)

2   tablespoons butter, melted

2   tablespoons olive oil

    Salt and pepper to taste

½   cup milk, warmed over low heat

1. Preheat the oven to 425°.

2. Wrap the whole garlic head in tin foil or place in a garlic roaster and roast for 1 hour or until garlic is just turning golden.

3. While the garlic is roasting, in a large pot bring 4 quarts of water and ½ teaspoon of salt to a boil. Add the potatoes and cook covered for 20 to 40 minutes until tender. Drain.

4. When the garlic is cool enough to handle, slice off just enough of the head to expose the cloves. Squeeze out the garlic into a small bowl and discard the skin. Add the butter, olive oil, salt, and pepper and mix well.

5. Transfer the potatoes to a large mixing bowl and mash with a potato masher or fork. Add the warmed milk and beat with a fork until well blended. Add the garlic mixture and beat until creamy. Serve immediately.

IGORISM:
Those aren't mashed potatoes, sir. It's congealed grease.

DINNER

Igor's Promotion Potato Cakes

Makes about 12 cakes

1	teaspoon salt, divided
1½	pounds russet potatoes (about 4 large), peeled and quartered
2	jalapeño peppers, seeded and minced
1	tablespoon fresh chopped cilantro
½	teaspoon ground cumin
½	teaspoon ground coriander
½	teaspoon grated fresh ginger
	Vegetable oil for frying

1. In a large pot bring 3 quarts of water and ½ teaspoon of salt to a boil. Add the potatoes and cook covered for 20 to 40 minutes until tender.

2. Drain the potatoes and transfer to a large mixing bowl. Mash with a potato masher or fork. Add the peppers, cilantro, cumin, coriander, and ginger, and mix thoroughly. Shape the mixture into thick round cakes, about 2 tablespoons for each, 3 inches in diameter.

3. In a large heavy skillet heat ¼ cup of oil over medium-high heat. Fry 3 to 4 potato cakes at a time for about 5 minutes or until golden brown and a light crust has formed. When the first side is browned, carefully lift with a spatula to flip over. Be gentle; they will be very soft in the middle. Brown the other side, then drain on paper towels. Add more oil as needed until all the cakes are cooked.

4. Place in a 250° oven to keep warm until all are done. Serve immediately.

DINNER

Slickee Boy Sweet Potatoes

Serves 6

2	pounds sweet potatoes, scrubbed and quartered
½	cup plain breadcrumbs
½	cup grated Parmesan cheese
2	teaspoons Italian seasoning
2	eggs, beaten well
½	teaspoon crushed red pepper flakes

1. Preheat the oven to 350°.

2. Slice the potatoes into ½-inch wedges and set aside.

3. In a shallow bowl combine the breadcrumbs, Parmesan, and Italian seasoning. Dip the potato wedges into the beaten eggs, then dredge in the breadcrumb mixture.

4. Arrange the potatoes on a lightly oiled baking pan and bake for 20 to 30 minutes or until tender. Turn once during baking. Sprinkle with red pepper flakes and serve immediately.

HOT LIPS: Frank, we've got hours.
FRANK: That's right, let the others get theirs.

• SECTION 8 •

M*A*S*H-ellaneous

Asparagus with Anchovy Salve

Serves 4 to 6

1½	pounds fresh asparagus spears, ends trimmed off
6	anchovy fillets, mashed
¾	cup mayonnaise
2	tablespoons sour cream
2	tablespoons chopped parsley
2	cloves garlic, minced
½	teaspoon freshly ground black pepper

1. In a large pot of boiling water steam the asparagus for 5 minutes or until tender-crisp. Rinse under cold water to stop cooking. Drain well and refrigerate.

2. In a small bowl combine the anchovies, mayonnaise, sour cream, parsley, garlic, and pepper. Mix until well blended. Refrigerate for at least 1 hour. Serve with chilled asparagus spears.

"I can't get to sleep unless I count sacrificial sheep."
—MULCAHY

Aspirator Asparagus Rolls

Serves 6 to 8

12	fresh asparagus spears, ends trimmed off
6	ounces blue cheese
1	ounce cream cheese
¼	cup mayonnaise
12	thin slices white bread
1	tablespoon chopped scallions
¼	cup unsalted butter, melted
½	cup grated romano cheese

1. Preheat the oven to 350°.

2. In a large pot of boiling water steam the asparagus for 5 minutes or until tender-crisp. Reserve.

3. In a food processor combine the blue cheese, cream cheese, and mayonnaise and process until smooth. Reserve.

4. Trim the crusts from the bread slices. With a rolling pin, roll each slice to ⅛-inch thick. Spread a thin layer of the cheese mixture on each slice, then sprinkle each with chopped scallions. Top with an asparagus spear and roll them up.

5. Brush each roll with melted butter. Roll them in the romano cheese until well coated.

6. Place the rolls on a baking sheet and bake for 15 minutes or until the cheese is golden brown. Remove and cut into halves. Serve immediately.

Attention All Personnel Pickle Chips

Serves 8 to 10

Peanut oil for deep frying

3   eggs

1   cup ice water

½   teaspoon baking powder

1½ cups all-purpose flour

½   teaspoon salt

1   large jar dill pickle chips, drained and patted dry

Salt to taste

1. In a deep heavy skillet heat 1 inch of peanut oil, enough to cover the dill chips, to 375°.

2. In a large bowl whisk together the eggs and ice water. Stir in the baking powder, flour, and salt. Do not overmix, the mixture should be lumpy.

3. Dip the dill chips into the batter to coat, then fry until golden brown. Add peanut oil as needed. Drain the chips on paper towels. Season with salt and serve.

IGOR: Peas or carrots, Sir?

HAWKEYE: Oh, a little of each will be fine.

IGOR: Good, because I don't know which is which.

Everybody seems to want something from the Colonel.

IGORISM:

Hawkeye told me he went to school for twelve years to be a doctor. I trained in boot camp for eight weeks to become a soldier. It sure takes a lot more time to learn how to save a life than how to end one.

Cheesey Eggplant Militaire

Serves 4

1	large eggplant, peeled and cut lengthwise into ½-inch slices
3	eggs, lightly beaten
2	cups whole milk
2	cups seasoned breadcrumbs
3	tablespoons olive oil
¾	cup Gorgonzola cheese, crumbled
	Salt and pepper
½	cup prepared marinara sauce
	Fresh Italian parsley

1. Soak the eggplant slices in cool water for 30 minutes.

2. In a medium mixing bowl combine the eggs and milk. Dip the eggplant slices in the egg and milk wash, then dredge them in the seasoned breadcrumbs.

3. In a sauté pan heat the olive oil over medium-high heat until oil just starts to smoke. Add the breaded eggplant and cook for 2½ minutes on each side.

4. Place the eggplant on a baking sheet and sprinkle with Gorgonzola cheese. Add salt and pepper to taste. Place under a broiler until the cheese melts. Transfer to individual serving plates and garnish each with a bullet of marinara and a sprig of parsley.

IGORISM:
If you want green, have the liver!

SECTION 8

Chopper Liver

Serves 2 to 4

2	tablespoons butter
1	pound chicken livers, sliced into halves
6	eggs, hard boiled, shelled, and finely chopped
1	medium onion, finely chopped
	Salt and pepper to taste
1	tablespoon rendered chicken fat

1. In a large skillet melt 2 tablespoons of butter over medium heat. Add the chicken livers and quickly sauté for about 1 minute on each side. Transfer to a bowl and let cool.

2. In a large mixing bowl combine the eggs and onion and mix well. Finely chop the chicken livers, then add them to the egg mixture. Season with salt and pepper, add the rendered chicken fat, and mix well. Cover and refrigerate for 1 hour to set. Remove from the refrigerator 15 to 20 minutes before serving.

A couple of good doctors.

Dear Ma,

I know everybody's got their own way about them, but this doctor, Major Winchester, has a stick up his...uh, I mean, he's just plain stuffy! He walks around with his nose up in the air like he's breathin' dif-ferent air than the rest of us. He looks at me like I'm a bug. Remember when my teacher, Mrs. Wilson, told you I had a bad attitude in class? Well the Major's got one of those too.

Don't get me wrong, Ma - he's a real-ly good surgeon, so if I ever need an operation I want him to mess with my innerds. He plays music I've never heard before - it has no beat to it at all. Thing is, I can't seem to get it out of my head. Maybe I'll ask him about it. I hope he doesn't try to step on me. Ha ha.

Love, Igor

Crab-Stuffed Pepper Grenades

Serves 6

1	cup cream cheese
½	cup ricotta cheese
½	cup fresh crab meat, picked over for shells and filament
12	large jalapeño peppers, with stems intact
1	large egg, beaten
2	tablespoons milk
1	tablespoon all-purpose flour
¼	cup grated Parmesan cheese
1¼	cups seasoned breadcrumbs
	Vegetable oil for frying

1. In a medium mixing bowl combine the cream cheese, ricotta cheese, and crab meat and mix well. Reserve.

2. Slice each pepper open, starting at the tip, just enough to remove the seeds and keep the stem attached. Stuff each pepper with crab and cheese mixture. Press the pepper back together and reserve.

3. In a small bowl mix together the egg, milk, and flour. In a shallow dish combine the Parmesan cheese and breadcrumbs. Dip each stuffed pepper in the egg mixture then roll them in the cheese and breadcrumbs until well coated. Secure the peppers with toothpicks if needed.

4. Place the peppers in the freezer for 30 minutes until set.

5. Heat the vegetable oil in a deep heavy skillet or deep fryer to 375°. Remove the peppers from the freezer and fry until golden brown. Drain on paper towels and serve.

General Reynolds' Directive Dip

Roasted Eggplant Dip

Makes about 2 cups

2	medium eggplants
¼	cup fresh lemon juice
2	tablespoons sesame tahini (found in the ethnic section)
4	cloves garlic, minced
1	tablespoon chopped fresh cilantro
1	teaspoon Tabasco sauce
⅛	teaspoon cayenne pepper
½	teaspoon salt
¼	teaspoon black pepper
	Fresh cilantro sprigs for garnish
1	large loaf pita bread, cut into wedges
	Assorted raw vegetables

1. Preheat the barbecue grill to medium-high.

2. Pierce the eggplants in several places with a fork. Grill the eggplants, covered, for 35 minutes or until the skin is blistered and blackened. Let cool. When cool enough to handle, peel off the skins. Allow the eggplants to cool further.

3. Chop eggplant pulps coarsely, then place in a food processor fitted with the steel blade. Add the lemon juice, tahini, garlic, cilantro, Tabasco, cayenne, salt, and pepper and process until smooth.

4. Refrigerate for 2 hours before serving. Garnish with fresh cilantro sprigs and serve with pita bread and crudités.

*Here's a shot of Captain Hunnicutt and Major Houlihan
thinkin' about something important.*

I told 'em to smile for my folks back home.

Hawkeye Pierce's Pickled Shrimp

Serves 6

½	cup olive oil
½	cup white wine
	Juice of 1 lemon
4	cloves garlic, minced
2	tablespoons fresh chopped basil
2	teaspoons Worcestershire sauce
⅛	teaspoon cayenne pepper
	Salt and freshly ground pepper to taste
2	pounds jumbo shrimp, peeled and deveined leaving tails intact

1. In a large shallow dish combine all of the above ingredients except the shrimp and mix well. Add the shrimp and toss gently to coat. Cover and refrigerate for 2 to 3 hours, stirring occasionally.

2. Preheat the broiler or barbecue to medium.

3. Drain the shrimp and discard the marinade. Grill or broil for 3 to 4 minutes on each side or just until the shrimp turn opaque. Transfer to a platter and serve immediately.

"Hey, Igor, keeper of the public ptomaine. Before you go to bed, don't forget to walk tomorrow's breakfast!"
—HAWKEYE

Incubator Shrimp

with Cayenne-Lemon Butter

Serves 6

For the Shrimp:

12	ounces beer
1	tablespoon crushed black peppercorns
1	tablespoon salt
1	tablespoon Tabasco sauce
2	pounds unpeeled jumbo shrimp

1. In a large heavy pot combine all of the above ingredients and bring to a boil. Reduce the heat, cover, and simmer for 15 minutes.

2. Remove the pan from the heat and transfer the shrimp and liquid to a large bowl. Refrigerate for 1 hour. Drain the shrimp and discard the marinade. Serve on a large platter with lots of napkins and lemon butter on the side.

For the Lemon Butter:

¾	cup clarified butter
1	tablespoon lemon juice
⅛	teaspoon cayenne pepper

In a saucepan heat the clarified butter over low heat slowly until light brown. Add lemon juice and cayenne pepper and serve.

Intravenous Drip Dip

Baked Deviled Crab Dip

Serves 6

½	cup mayonnaise
3	tablespoons Heinz chili sauce
2	tablespoons grated Parmesan cheese
2	teaspoons fresh lemon juice
1½	teaspoons Dijon mustard
1½	teaspoons Worcestershire sauce
¼	teaspoon cayenne pepper
	Salt and freshly ground black pepper to taste
2	cups fresh crab meat, picked over for shell or filament
½	cup grated Gruyère cheese
	Toast sticks and small toast rounds for dipping

1. Preheat the oven to 325°.

2. In a large mixing bowl combine the mayonnaise, chili sauce, Parmesan, lemon juice, Dijon mustard, Worcestershire sauce, cayenne pepper, salt, and pepper and mix well. Add the crab meat and stir until well blended.

3. Transfer to a shallow, ovenproof serving dish and sprinkle on the Gruyère cheese. Bake for 10 to 15 minutes or until heated through and the cheese melts and begins to brown. Serve hot with toast sticks and rounds.

Jeep Jerky

3	pounds lean meat, flank steak or brisket
1½	teaspoons seasoned salt
½	teaspoon lemon pepper
½	teaspoon garlic powder
¼	cup soy sauce
½	cup Worcestershire sauce
¼	teaspoon red pepper flakes

1. Trim the meat of all fat. Place between 2 sheets of waxed paper and pound with a meat mallet to tenderize.

   Optional: Secure the meat in a clean durable cloth and back over it several times with a jeep to tenderize. Place in a dish large enough to lay the meat flat.

2. In a small bowl mix the remaining ingredients. Pour the marinade over the meat, cover, and refrigerate for 12 to 24 hours.

3. Preheat the oven to 175°.

4. Slice the meat as thinly as possible into ¼- to ½-inch strips—with the grain for chewiness or against the grain for tenderness. Place the strips of meat on a wire rack in the oven so that the meat does not overlap and bake for 10 or 12 hours. Test often. It should be leathery and tough, but not break when bent. Store in an airtight container.

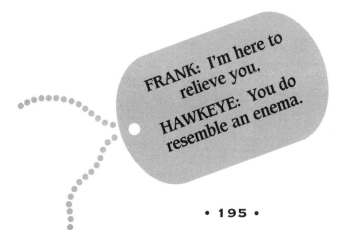

FRANK: I'm here to relieve you,

HAWKEYE: You do resemble an enema.

SECTION 8

Captain Pierce likes to study the food before he eats it.

"Is it treason
to refuse to serve
liver tartare?"
—B.J.

M*A*S*H Liver Tartare

Serves 6 to 8

8	ounces liverwurst
¼	cup sour cream
1	tablespoon mayonnaise
½	teaspoon A.1. Steak Sauce
	Dash of Tabasco sauce
	Chopped parsley for garnish

1. In a blender combine all of the ingredients except the parsley and mix until smooth.

2. Spoon onto a sheet of waxed paper and roll the pâté into a log shape. Sprinkle with parsley then chill for 1 hour or until firm.

3. Transfer the pâté to a serving dish, cut into ½-inch slices, and serve.

IGOR: What's that? You can't make up words.

HAWKEYE: I didn't. It's an electrical musical instrument.
They use it in movies. Your turn.

IGOR: I don't want to play anymore. It's stupid.
You're killing me. My best word was pig. And you
only let me use one 'g.'

Mildred Potter's Spinach Rolls

Serves 6 to 8

For the Spinach:

1	pound fresh spinach, thoroughly washed and stems removed
¼	cup sour cream
1	teaspoon horseradish
⅛	teaspoon Dijon mustard
	Salt and pepper to taste

Add the spinach leaves to 2 cups of rapidly boiling water. Reduce the heat and simmer covered until tender, about 8 minutes. Drain the spinach well. Transfer to a blender or food processor and add the sour cream, horseradish, Dijon mustard, salt, and pepper. Process briefly and set aside.

For the Sautéed Mushrooms:

2	tablespoons butter
1	tablespoon olive oil
2	cloves garlic, minced
1	pound fresh mushroom caps, sliced

In a large skillet heat the butter and olive oil over medium-high heat. Add the garlic and sauté for 1 minute. Add the mushroom slices and sauté for 3 to 4 minutes. Transfer to a dish and set aside.

For the Pancakes:

¾	cup all-purpose flour
2	tablespoons sugar

1   teaspoon baking powder

1   teaspoon salt

2   eggs, beaten

¾   cup milk

¼   cup water

¾   teaspoon vanilla extract

     Vegetable oil

¾   cup grated Gruyère cheese

1. Sift the flour into a mixing bowl. Add the sugar, baking powder, and salt, and sift again. In a separate bowl combine the eggs, milk, water, and vanilla and beat well. Make a well in the center of the dry ingredients and pour in the liquid ingredients. Mix together with just a few quick strokes. Lumps are OK.

2. Heat a lightly oiled skillet over medium heat. Add about 2 tablespoons of batter per pancake. Tip the skillet slightly to allow the batter to spread to a 5-inch diameter. When it is brown underneath, flip the pancake and brown the other side. Add oil as needed until all the cakes are done.

3. Preheat the broiler. Place a little spinach and mushrooms on each pancake. Roll them up and place them seam-side down on an ovenproof platter. Sprinkle the tops with grated Gruyère cheese. Place under the broiler for 5 minutes or until the cheese is melted. Serve immediately.

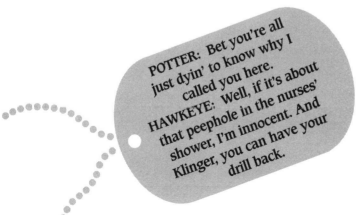

POTTER: Bet you're all just dyin' to know why I called you here.
HAWKEYE: Well, if it's about that peephole in the nurses' shower, I'm innocent. And Klinger, you can have your drill back.

Movie Night Popcorn Shrimp

with Sweet and Sour Pineapple Sauce

Serves 4 to 6

For the Shrimp:

	Vegetable oil for deep frying
1½	cups all-purpose flour
1	teaspoon baking powder
½	teaspoon salt
2	eggs, beaten
1	cup cold beer
1	pound medium shrimp, shelled and deveined

1. In a deep fryer or deep heavy skillet heat enough oil to cover the shrimp to 375°.

2. In a large bowl sift together flour, baking powder, and salt. Stir in the eggs and beer. Do not overmix; the mixture should be lumpy.

3. Dip the shrimp into the batter to coat, then fry until golden brown. Add oil as needed. Drain the shrimp on paper towels. Serve with Pineapple Sauce (recipe follows).

For the Sauce:

2	tablespoons cornstarch
1	tablespoon brown sugar
1	teaspoon soy sauce
½	teaspoon black pepper
⅛	cup mild vinegar
½	cup pineapple juice
1	cup crushed canned pineapple

1. In a small bowl combine the cornstarch, brown sugar, soy sauce, pepper, and vinegar.

2. In a medium saucepan heat the pineapple juice over medium heat. Stir in the vinegar mixture and crushed pineapple and bring to a boil briefly. Reduce the heat and simmer, stirring constantly, until the mixture thickens. Remove from the heat and let cool slightly before serving.

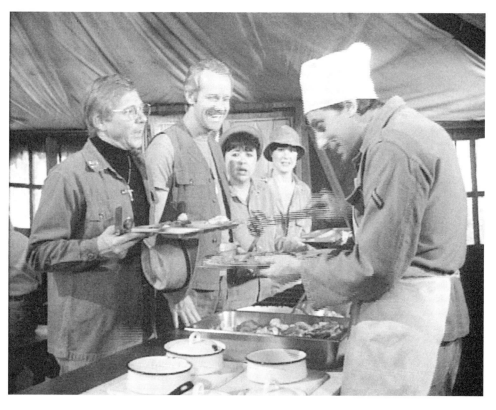

Them were really good peas I was servin.'

Nurse Sherie's Crusty Crostini

with Tomato Pesto and Mozzarella

Serves 4 to 6

1	8-ounce jar oil-packed sun-dried tomatoes, undrained
4	cloves garlic, chopped
½	cup chopped kalamata olives
1	small loaf Italian bread, cut into 12 slices
2	tablespoons unsalted butter, softened
	Freshly ground black pepper to taste
4	tablespoons chopped fresh basil
10	ounces water-packed mozzarella cheese, shredded

1. In the bowl of a food processor combine the tomatoes in oil and garlic. Process until smooth. Transfer the mixture to a medium bowl. Mix in the chopped olives and set aside.

2. Preheat the broiler.

3. Lightly butter both sides of each slice of bread. Heat a heavy skillet over medium heat and sauté the bread slices until light brown on both sides. Spread about 2 tablespoons of the tomato mixture over each slice. Place the slices on an oven-proof platter.

4. Top each crostini with chopped basil and freshly ground pepper, and cover with shredded mozzarella. Place under the broiler for 3 to 4 minutes or until the cheese begins to melt and is lightly browned. Cut into quarters and serve.

R & R Hot Crab Dip

Serves 4 to 6

1   7½-ounce can crab meat, drained and picked over for shells
1   8-ounce package cream cheese, at room temperature
1   tablespoon horseradish
2   tablespoons heavy cream
3   tablespoons prepared chili sauce
    Salt to taste

1. Preheat the oven to 350°.

2. In a medium mixing bowl combine all of the ingredients. Transfer to an oven-proof serving dish and bake for 15 minutes.

3. Remove from the oven and let stand for 5 to 10 minutes before serving.

Serve with fresh vegetable crudités and crusty bread.

Some of the gang hangin' around in the mess tent.

Red Alert Tortillas

Serves 6 to 8

1	8-ounce package cream cheese, room temperature
6	jalapeño peppers, seeded and chopped
3	cloves garlic, minced
½	teaspoon vegetable seasoning
⅛	teaspoon ground cumin
12	small flour tortillas, room temperature

1. Preheat the oven to 350°.

2. In the bowl of a food processor fitted with the steel blade process the cream cheese, peppers, and seasonings until smooth.

3. Spread about 1 tablespoon of the cheese mixture over each of the tortillas. Roll the tortillas tightly. Refrigerate for at least 2 hours.

4. Cut the rolled tortillas into thirds. Place on a baking sheet and bake for 10 to 15 minutes or until lightly browned. Transfer to a platter and serve immediately.

HOT LIPS: Have a good trip, men.

HAWKEYE: How about a little kiss for the road?

HOT LIPS: Don't be ridiculous.

HAWKEYE: Then how about one for me?

SECTION 8

Sweet and Sour Stretcher Shrimp

Serves 3 to 4

4	teaspoons sugar
4½	tablespoons vinegar
4½	teaspoons shoyu (Japanese soy sauce)
4½	ounces small bay shrimp, shelled and cooked

1. In a small mixing bowl combine the sugar, vinegar, and shoyu. Add the shrimp to the marinade, cover, and refrigerate for at least 2 hours, preferably overnight.

2. Drain the shrimp well and discard the marinade. Serve as a side dish or as an appetizer by placing 2 to 3 shrimp at a time on toothpicks and serving on a chilled platter.

Everybody's listening to a baseball game on the radio.

Adrenaline Rush Brownies

Makes about 12 brownies

1½	cups unsalted butter
8	ounces semisweet chocolate chips
8	ounces unsweetened chocolate, chopped
6	large eggs
3	tablespoons espresso coffee powder
2	tablespoons vanilla extract
1¾	cups sugar
1¼	cups sifted all-purpose flour
1	tablespoon baking powder
⅛	teaspoon cayenne pepper
8	ounces white chocolate chips

1. Preheat the oven to 350°.

2. Butter and flour a 9 x 13-inch baking pan and set aside.

3. In the top of a double boiler over simmering water melt together the butter, semi-sweet chocolate chips, and unsweetened chocolate and stir until smooth. Remove from the heat and let cool.

4. In a large mixing bowl whisk together the eggs, espresso, vanilla, and sugar until fluffy. Stir in the cooled chocolate and reserve.

5. Sift together the flour, baking powder, and cayenne pepper. Mix into the batter, then fold in the white chocolate chips. Pour into the buttered pan and bake for 25 to 30 minutes. Cool slightly then cut into squares.

Dear Ma,

Holy Moly, there are so many different kinds of people in the world. I've seen Koreans, Turks, Australians, Greeks, Chinese and a bunch of others. No matter what color they are or where they come from, it seems like everybody just wants to eat good food and go home to their families. Too bad they have to eat here. Ha ha.

I know you didn't know I knew, but I know about Uncle Irwin. See, there's a guy here just like him, only he does it to get out of the Army. When I first saw Klinger dressed up like Auntie Bobbie, I thought he was nuts and wouldn't go near him. After watching this war, though, he just didn't seem so crazy any more. Okay, he may act a little funny, but it really doesn't make any difference what somebody looks like or how they dress. We're all just people underneath our duds. Maybe 'cause I'm family, but Uncle Irwin's a lot prettier than Klinger. Ha ha.

Love, Igor

P.S. Don't tell Janine, but I bought something from Klinger that she's gonna look like a million bucks in. If she doesn't like it, I'll give it to you know who!

Bombshell Bananas

Brandied Banana Fritters

Serves 4

4	ripe bananas (not mushy), peeled and cut into 4 diagonal pieces
½	cup brandy
2	egg yolks
1	cup milk
1	tablespoon butter, melted
1	cup sifted all-purpose flour
⅛	teaspoon salt
½	tablespoon sugar
	Vegetable oil for frying
	Confectioners' sugar for dusting
	Vanilla ice cream
½	cup semisweet chocolate chips

1. In a shallow bowl combine the sliced bananas and brandy. Toss to coat well, then cover and refrigerate for 2 hours.

2. In a medium mixing bowl beat together the egg yolks, milk, and butter. In a separate bowl sift together the flour, salt, and sugar. Add the liquid ingredients to the dry and mix. Cover and refrigerate for 2 hours.

3. After 2 hours, heat vegetable oil in a deep fat fryer or frying pan to 375°. With an electric mixer beat the dough well until smooth.

4. Drain the bananas well. Dust with confectioners' sugar, then dip the slices into the batter. Fry for 3 to 5 minutes or until golden brown. Drain on paper towels. Dust with confectioners' sugar.

5. In a small saucepan melt the chocolate chips . Place a generous scoop of ice cream into individual bowls. Divide the banana fritters among the bowls. Drizzle melted chocolate over the top and serve.

Bug-Out Brownies

Makes about 20 brownies

1	cup unsalted butter
2	cups semisweet chocolate chips, divided
4	ounces unsweetened chocolate
3	eggs, room temperature
1	tablespoon instant espresso
2	cups sugar
1	tablespoon vanilla extract
2	tablespoons Chambord (raspberry liqueur)
¾	cup sifted all-purpose flour
1½	teaspoons baking powder
½	teaspoon salt

1. Preheat the oven to 350°. Grease and flour a 9 x 13-inch pan.

2. In the top of a double boiler over simmering water melt and stir the butter, 1 cup of chocolate chips, and the unsweetened chocolate until smooth. Cool the mixture to room temperature.

3. In a large bowl combine the eggs, espresso, sugar, vanilla, and raspberry liqueur. Add the cooled chocolate mixture, using a few swift strokes to blend. Do not overmix.

4. In a separate bowl combine the flour, baking powder, and salt. Gently stir the dry ingredients into the chocolate mixture. Fold in the remaining chocolate chips. Pour the batter into the greased pan and bake for about 25 minutes. Cool thoroughly. Cut into squares and serve with vanilla ice cream.

Charles' Blueblood Berry Cake

with Lemon Frosting

Serves 8

For the Cake:

½   cup shortening

1   cup sugar

2   eggs

2   cups sifted all-purpose flour

4   teaspoons baking powder

½   teaspoon salt

1   teaspoon grated nutmeg

1   cup milk

2   cups fresh blueberries

1. Preheat the oven to 375°. Grease two 9- or 10-inch layer-cake pans.

2. In a large mixing bowl, beat the shortening with an electric mixer until smooth then add the sugar and beat until creamy. Add the eggs and beat until light and foamy.

3. In a separate large mixing bowl sift together the flour, baking powder, salt, and nutmeg. Add the flour to the creamed mixture ½ cup at time, alternating with ¼ cup of milk each time until smooth.

4. Gently fold the blueberries into the batter. Pour into the prepared pans and bake for 25 to 30 minutes. When done, the cake should be lightly browned and beginning to shrink from the sides of the pan.

5. Remove from the oven and allow to cool for 10 minutes in the pans, then turn onto cake racks.

For the Frosting:

½   cup butter or margarine, softened

1   pound confectioners' sugar, sifted

1   teaspoon grated lemon rind

¼   cup fresh lemon juice

1. In a large mixing bowl, combine the above ingredients and beat with an electric mixer until smooth.

2. Transfer one cake layer top side down onto a plate. If you are working directly on the serving platter, tuck waxed paper under the edge of the cake to catch spillage, then remove after applying the frosting.

3. Spoon on about one-fourth to one-third of the frosting as filling and smooth with a spatula. Add the other cake layer, spoon the remaining frosting on top and slather around the sides.

Celebratin' over who won the game.

Colonel Gelbart's Eloquent
Cream of Peanut Cheesecake

Serves 8 to 10

For the Crust:

25	Oreo cookies (2½ cups crumbs)
¼	cup unsalted butter, melted

1. Preheat the oven to 325°.

2. Place the cookies and butter in the bowl of a food processor fitted with the steel blade and process until the crumbs are uniform. Pour the crumbs into the bottom of an 8-inch springform mold. Press evenly over the bottom and about halfway up the sides. Refrigerate.

For the Filling:

2	8-ounce packages cream cheese, at room temperature
4	large eggs, at room temperature
1	cup sugar
¾	cup creamy peanut butter
1	cup semisweet chocolate chips
½	cup sour cream
2	tablespoons Kahlua

1. In a large bowl combine the cream cheese, eggs, and sugar and beat with an electric mixer on medium speed until light and fluffy, about 4 minutes. Add the peanut butter and mix well. Add the chocolate chips, sour cream, and Kahlua and mix thoroughly.

2. Pour the batter into the springform pan. Place on a baking sheet and bake for 1 hour or until the sides are firm and the center is slightly soft.

3. At the end of the baking time, turn off the heat and open the oven door slightly. Allow the cake to cool in the oven for 20 minutes before removing. Remove to a wire rack and cool to room temperature. Cover with plastic wrap and refrigerate for at least 6 hours. The cheesecake can be prepared up to 3 days ahead.

4. Remove the cheesecake from the refrigerator 10 minutes before serving. Remove the sides of the springform and serve.

It's hard to recognize the Colonel under all that beard.

I made Captain Pierce his favorite dessert—Strawberry Shortcake with real *strawberries.*

Crabapple Cove Blueberry Buckle

Serves 4 to 6

½   cup shortening

½   cup sugar

1   egg, beaten

2   cups all-purpose flour

½   teaspoon salt

2½   teaspoons baking powder

½   cup milk

2½   cups fresh frozen blueberries

½   cup sugar

½   cup all-purpose flour

¾   teaspoon ground cinnamon

¼   cup butter or margarine

1. Preheat the oven to 375°. Grease an 8-inch square pan.

2. Using an electric mixer, cream the shortening and ½ cup of sugar. Add the egg and mix well.

3. In a separate bowl mix and sift 2 cups of flour, salt, and baking powder together. Add the sifted ingredients to the creamed mixture in about 3 parts, alternately with the milk. Spread the dough in the prepared pan. Spread the blueberries over the top of the dough.

4. In a small bowl mix and sift together ½ cup of sugar, ½ cup of flour, and the ground cinnamon. Cut in ¼ cup of butter or margarine. Sprinkle this mixture over the top of the blueberries. Bake for 1 hour to 1 hour and 15 minutes.

5. Serve warm as a coffee cake or as a dessert with vanilla ice cream. To rewarm, place in a paper bag and sprinkle the bag with water; place in a warm oven until the buckle is thoroughly heated.

Forward Marsh Melts

Serves 4

16   Ritz crackers

      Peanut butter

      Chocolate chips

16   marshmallows

      Jam (strawberry/raspberry)

1. Preheat the oven to 350°.

2. Spread a generous amount of peanut butter on a Ritz cracker. Drop a few chocolate chips on the peanut butter and top with a marshmallow.

3. Place crackers on a baking sheet and bake until the marshmallow begins to melt and turn golden brown on top. (If it turns black, start over).

4. Remove from the oven and serve with a dollop of strawberry or raspberry jam.

Looks like hand signals at a football game. Ha ha.

GI Java Joe Jello

Coffee Gelatin with Vanilla Whipped Cream

Serves 4

1	tablespoon plain gelatin powder
¼	cup cold water
6	tablespoons sugar
⅛	teaspoon salt
1¾	cups hot strong coffee
1	cup whipping cream
½	teaspoon vanilla extract
2	tablespoons sifted confectioners' sugar

1. Soak the gelatin in cold water for 5 minutes. Add the sugar, salt, and coffee and mix well. Chill until firm.

2. In a large chilled bowl beat the cream with an electric beater on medium-high speed until the cream begins to thicken. Then, lower the speed and whip just to the point where soft peaks form.

3. Fold in the vanilla and confectioners' sugar. Spoon over the coffee gelatin and serve immediately.

FLAGG: I have no home. I'm the wind.

HAWKEYE: I told you he was the wind. You said he was the stars.

B.J.: I said he was the moon.

Henry Blake's Chocolate Cake

Serves 6 to 8

For the Cake:

1	tablespoon all-purpose flour
3	cups sugar
1½	cups cocoa
1½	cups corn oil
3	cups water
3½	cups all-purpose flour, sifted
1½	teaspoons vanilla extract
4	ounces semisweet chocolate chips

1. Preheat the oven to 350°. Spray two 9-inch cake pans with vegetable oil spray. Dust each pan with 1½ teaspoons of flour, coating the bottom and sides evenly. Remove the excess by overturning the pan and gently tapping.

2. In a large mixing bowl stir together the sugar and cocoa. Add the oil and mix thoroughly. With an electric mixer on low, alternately add the water and flour in thirds, mixing until the batter is smooth. Mix in the vanilla.

3. Pour the batter into the prepared cake pans. Sprinkle chocolate chips evenly on top of each cake batter. Bake for 40 to 50 minutes. Remove from the oven and allow to cool for 10 minutes in the pans, then turn onto wire cake racks.

For the Frosting:

1	cup butter, softened
1	cup cocoa
5	cups confectioners' sugar
½	teaspoon vanilla extract
6	tablespoons milk

1. In the bowl of a food processor fitted with the steel blade combine the butter and cocoa. Process until mixed. With the machine still running, add the confectioners' sugar and vanilla. Add the milk 1 tablespoon at a time and process until the mixture is fluffy.

2. Transfer one cake layer, top side down, to a plate. If you are working directly on the serving platter, tuck waxed paper under the edge of the cake to catch spillage, then remove after applying the frosting.

3. Spoon on about one-fourth to one-third of the frosting as filling and smooth with a spatula. Add the other cake layer, spoon the remaining frosting on top, and slather around the sides.

This is us tryin' to have a Happy New Year.

Dear Ma,

Remember how long it took us to get that stuff to kill the termites? I'll never forget the expression on Pop's face when it finally arrived — one day after the fence crashed on top of the Ford. If we had only known Radar then, Pop wouldn't have had to repaint the car. Ha ha.

Radar is the Colonel's clerk who does everything the Colonel needs done to keep the camp runnin' smooth. Everybody here needs supplies of all kinds and Radar knows just how to get 'em. Corporal O'Reilly is his real name, but we call him Radar because he can tell when the choppers are comin' way before any of us can see or hear 'em. He even knows what the Colonel's gonna say before he says it. Wierd, huh?

You know how I never cared much for critters. Well, Radar keeps rabbits and skunks for pets. I don't believe I'm sayin' this, but they're really kind of cute. Janine will be happy to hear that I made a promise to Radar never to shoot anything furry again. But I never said anything about not shootin' termites. Ha ha.

Love, Igor

Hunnicut's Homesick Cookies

Makes about 36 cookies

½   cup chunky-style peanut butter, room temperature

½   cup unsalted butter, softened

½   cup firmly packed brown sugar

⅓   cup sugar

1   large egg

1   teaspoon vanilla extract

2   cups sifted all-purpose flour

½   teaspoon salt

1   teaspoon baking soda

¼   cup milk

1   cup semisweet chocolate chips

15   frozen miniature peanut butter cups, coarsely chopped

1. Preheat the oven to 375°.

2. In a large mixing bowl beat the peanut butter and butter until fluffy. Add the brown sugar and sugar gradually and beat until creamy. Add the egg and vanilla and beat for 2 to 3 minutes.

3. In a separate bowl combine the flour, salt, and baking soda. Add the flour mixture in 3 parts to the peanut butter mixture alternately with the milk. Beat the batter until smooth after each addition. Stir in the chocolate chips, then carefully fold in the peanut butter cup pieces.

4. Drop the batter in heaping tablespoons well apart onto an ungreased cookie sheet. Bake until lightly browned, about 12 minutes.

Major Metcalfe's Mousse

Frozen White Chocolate Mousse with Raspberry Sauce

Serves 8

For the Crust:

1	cup graham crackers crumbs
¼	cup unsalted butter, melted

1. Preheat the oven to 350°.
2. Place the graham cracker crumbs in the bottom of an 8-inch springform pan. Pour the melted butter over the crumbs and mix with a fork until well blended. Press the mixture firmly onto the bottom of the pan. Bake for 8 minutes. Cool on a wire rack and reserve.

For the Chocolate Mousse:

1	pound white chocolate, chopped
1½	cups whipping cream
6	tablespoons light rum
2½	cups chilled whipping cream

1. In a food processor finely chop the white chocolate.
2. In a large heavy saucepan bring 1½ cups of whipping cream to a boil. Reduce the heat and simmer for 2 to 3 minutes. Add the chocolate and stir until the chocolate is melted and the mixture is smooth. Transfer to a bowl and cool to room temperature. Stir the rum into the cooled chocolate mixture.
3. Pour 2½ cups of chilled cream into a chilled mixing bowl. Using an electric mixer, whip the cream until soft peaks form. Add one-third of the whipped cream to the chocolate mixture and fold to combine. Gently fold in the remaining cream. Pour into the crust and smooth the top. Cover the mousse with plastic wrap and freeze for at least 24 hours.

4. Remove the mousse from the freezer. Remove the springform sides, cut into wedges, and serve with raspberry sauce (below).

For the Raspberry Sauce:

1   10-ounce package frozen raspberries in syrup, thawed

Place a small strainer over a bowl. Pour in the raspberries and push through with a wooden spoon. Discard the seeds. Refrigerate until ready to use.

When I give a speech—everybody listens!

Peg's Pecan Pie

Serves 8 to 10

3	eggs, beaten
1½	teaspoons vanilla extract
1	cup light corn syrup
1	cup sugar
2	tablespoons butter, melted
2	generous cups pecans, reserving several unbroken pecans for the top
1	8-inch uncooked pie crust

1. Preheat the oven to 425°.

2. In a large mixing bowl combine the eggs, vanilla, corn syrup, sugar, butter, and pecans. Pour into the uncooked pie crust then decorate the top with whole pecans.

3. Bake for 10 minutes on the bottom rack of the oven, then reduce the temperature to 350° and bake for 45 to 50 minutes. Remove and cool for 30 minutes before serving.

4. Using a very sharp knife, cut small pieces. This is a very rich dessert.

There was something strange in that box.

Turkish Troop Cake

Serves 6 to 8

3	cups all-purpose flour
3	teaspoons baking powder
1	teaspoon salt
¾	cup poppy seeds
1½	cups canola oil
2	cups sugar
1	cup milk
1	teaspoon vanilla extract
4	eggs

1. Preheat the oven to 350°. Grease two 9-inch loaf pans or 1 bundt pan.

2. In a large mixing bowl combine the flour, baking powder, salt, and poppy seeds and set aside.

3. In a separate large mixing bowl combine the oil and the sugar and beat with electric mixer until smooth. Gradually pour in the milk. Add the vanilla and the eggs, one at a time, and beat well.

4. Add the dry ingredients and stir just to combine. Do not overmix. Pour the batter into the prepared pans and bake for 1 hour.

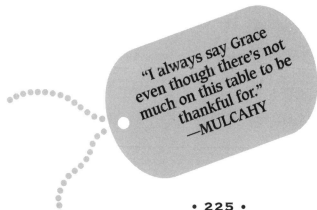

"I always say Grace even though there's not much on this table to be thankful for."
—MULCAHY

Captain Pierce asking me to dance. Just kiddin'—ha ha.

"Ambush Stew. It'll attack you
when you least expect it."
—B.J.

BARTENDER'S BEST SHOTS

Colonel Flagg's Truth Serum

Chocolate Cappucino

Serves 4

½	cup milk
½	cup half and half
2	ounces semisweet chocolate, finely chopped
2	teaspoons sugar
½	teaspoon vanilla extract
1	cup freshly brewed espresso coffee
¼	cup brandy
¼	cup light rum

1. In a large, heavy saucepan bring the milk and half and half to a simmer over medium heat. Pour into a blender. Add the chocolate, sugar, and vanilla. Cover and blend on low until the chocolate melts and the mixture is foamy.

2. Pour one-fourth of the espresso coffee in each of 4 cups. Add 1 tablespoon of brandy and 1 tablespoon of light rum to each cup. Add the hot chocolate, mix, and serve.

RADAR: What about your scorpions, sir?
FLAGG: That's okay, I'll get some from home.

General Jerry's Bloody Mary

Serves 1 to 6

1	32-ounce bottle Beefamato juice
2	cups vodka
¼	cup olive juice
2	tablespoons Tabasco sauce
2	tablespoons Worcestershire sauce
1	beef bouillon cube, dissolved in ¼ cup water
1½	teaspoons coarse horseradish
½	teaspoon black pepper
½	teaspoon salt
	Celery stalks and olives for garnish

In a large pitcher mix all of the ingredients together and serve on the rocks with celery and olives.

"It's sooo good, it makes a bulldog hug a hound!"

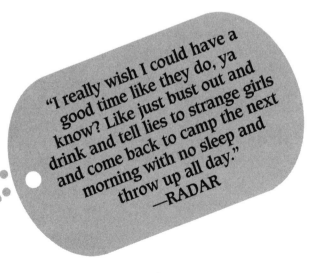

"I really wish I could have a good time like they do, ya know? Like just bust out and drink and tell lies to strange girls and come back to camp the next morning with no sleep and throw up all day."
—RADAR

Nurse Sherie's Creamed Whiskey

Irish Cream

Makes 1 blender full

1	cup whiskey
⅓	cup light rum
1	pint half and half
3	eggs or the equivalent egg substitute
1	teaspoon vanilla extract
2	tablespoons chocolate syrup
1	14-ounce can Eagle Brand sweetened condensed milk

Combine all of the ingredients in a blender and mix for 30 seconds. Cover and refrigerate for up to 3 weeks.

This drink is best if made 1 to 2 days in advance.

HOT LIPS: I thought you might enjoy being the Charity Officer for me. You'd be so good at it.

B.J.: Oh, really?

HOT LIPS: You have such a nice smile. Not liking you is the same as not liking a collie.

Dear Ma,

The camp decided to have a big picnic to celebrate the Fourth of July. Remember me telling you about the Chaplain, Father Mulcahy? He's a really nice guy. A'course, if he wasn't who would be, right? Ha ha. He heard me talkin' about the problem I was having with Janine, and says I should look in my heart and remember why I liked her in the first place. Anyway, he grew a bunch of corn and was excited about sharing it with everybody for the Fourth. At the party, the Father got real mad at me when he found out that all the corn was in cream and not still on the cob. I was mad because he didn't thank me for working so hard on all those ears. Later, he told me Priests are human, too, and we apologized to each other. Even said he liked the "mushy stuff." Ha ha.

Love, Igor

P.S. Oh yeah, if you see Miranda, tell her she should be happy with Morton and I won't be writing to her anymore.

Pre-Op Novocaine Shake

Serves 4

1	cup brandy
1	cup milk
¼	cup Kahlua
2	tablespoons chocolate ice cream
1	tablespoon vanilla extract
6	ice cubes

In a blender combine all of the ingredients and blend on high until smooth. Pour into glasses and serve.

Every once in a while I have a glug behind the bar.

Suicide Is Painless

Serves 1

	Ice
2	ounces sweet and sour
½	ounce vodka
½	ounce gin
½	ounce Triple Sec
½	ounce Tequila
½	ounce light rum
	Grape Nehi
	Lemon slice

Fill a 10- to 12-ounce mixing glass with ice. Add sweet and sour and liquors and shake to blend. Strain into a collins glass filled with ice cubes. Fill with Grape Nehi. Serve with a slice of lemon, a straw, and an iced tea spoon. Be careful operating heavy machinery—or anything else.

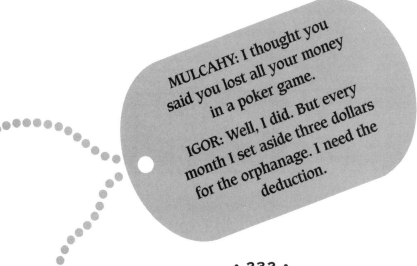

MULCAHY: I thought you said you lost all your money in a poker game.

IGOR: Well, I did. But every month I set aside three dollars for the orphanage. I need the deduction.

SECTION 8

Swamp Swill Martini

Serves 2

    Ice cubes

2   jiggers extra dry vermouth

4   jiggers vodka or gin

    Chilled martini glasses

    Jalapeño-stuffed olives for garnish

1. Fill a glass, cocktail shaker, or bedpan to the top with ice cubes. Pour vermouth over the ice, cover, and shake slowly for about 5 to 7 seconds.

2. Strain all the vermouth out of the container and immediately pour the vodka or gin over the vermouth-coated ice. Cover the container and slowly shake again for 5 to 7 seconds.

3. Strain into the chilled martini glasses. Drop in an olive or two and say Ahhhhh.

Captain McIntyre mixes with surgical precision.

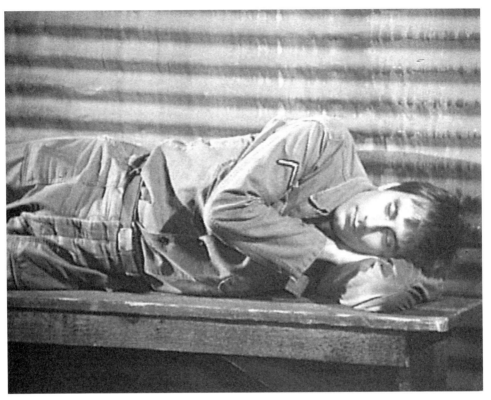

When you work as hard as I do, you take a snooze where you can.

IGORISM:
The beans? I wouldn't give 'em to my neighbor's dog.
In fact, they're so old, they're has beans.

MA!

I'm sure you've heard the news...IT"S OVER! I'll probably be home by the time you get this letter, but I wanted to write it anyway. Now that I'm comin' home, I'll tell you it's been really hard here. I've seen things that I hope nobody ever has to see again. The only thing that made it bearable were all the people who made this MASH what it is. I will miss them. Well, most of them. Ha ha. See you real soon!

Love, Igor

P.S. I'll make everybody dinner when I get there, but could somebody else please serve it? Ha ha.

• HOW I BECAME IGOR •

BY JEFF MAXWELL

Roll 'em

An actor's career in television usually begins with a nerve-jolting, gut-wrenching process known as an audition. The next Alan Alda or Loretta Swit is asked to perform a small portion of the script for a preliminary decision-maker known as a casting director. If the actor impresses, he or she gets a call back—to read for the producers and director. A final decision is made, and the telephone of one lucky auditionee rings with the sweet sound of employment.

My TV career, however, had wackier roots. Tense auditions and power lunches were replaced by a crowded bowling alley in Los Angeles. It was there that teams of bowlers from the famous movie studio, 20th Century Fox, met weekly to match their skills against other competitors. As general manager of Pico Bowl, my father was responsible for developing its profitable league business and, knowing that his kid wanted to be a "movie star," he convinced one of the bowling Fox execs that employing me would guarantee "special treatment" for his team. I don't know if anybody went on to win a trophy, but I was awarded a job!

For the next few days, I pressed my Dad for the glamorous details. All he could tell me, though, was that the job had "something to do with scripts." Okay, so it wasn't the movie-star position I had sought, but "something to do with scripts" couldn't be all that far off. Or could it?

Cut to eager young Maxwell pulling up to the fabled studios for his first day of work. A stone-faced guard slapped a pink sticker on the windshield, waived my VW Bug through the front gate—and into movie land. WOW-WEE! No more than twenty feet in front of me, I watched in awe as Cary Grant stepped out of his chauffeur-driven Rolls Royce and sauntered casually (just like he did on screen) across the street. Even my near head-on collision with a studio truck couldn't faze me. I had arrived!

Considering that I was about to work with screenplays, it made perfect sense that my new boss, Art, would introduce himself as head of the Print Department. Though I may have been a novice, even I knew that a script wasn't a script without any print on it. A friendly, jovial fellow, Art lavished praise on my father's generosity and welcomed this opportunity to reciprocate by bringing me "on board."

Finally, the big moment arrived: Art was ready to show me my office. Let's go! Can't wait to get started! The next thing I know, I'm following Art down a narrow hallway cluttered with random piles of 8½x11 sheets of paper. No Cary Grant; no exciting sound stages; no fancy dressing rooms in sight. Just a door at the end of the hall and the rapidly growing sound of pounding motors, along with acrid smells of gasoline, paint thinner and sweat. When we reached the door, Art smiled proudly. "This," he

HOW I BECAME IGOR

High School kid, Jeff Maxwell, meets his comedic idol, Jerry Lewis, on the set of his movie "The Family Jewels." I look like a folk-singer.

announced, "is where you're going to work." In one fell swoop, Art swung open the door and simultaneously slammed it shut on my Hollywood fantasy. Crammed end-to-end, in a room slightly larger than a school bus, were several printing presses roughly the size of medium rhinoceroses. Hunched over each one was a bedraggled, profusely-sweating human being. The floor, doubling as a trash can, was "carpeted" in a thick layer of paper strewn everywhere. It was then that the harried manager of this little operation, Freeman, frantically burst into the room, bellowed at the top of his lungs, "Hurrrrrrrrrry!" and quickly disappeared.

With a dry mouth and faltering voice, I shared my immediate concerns with Art. "Ah, don't worry," he said, reassuringly, "Once you learn the machines and Freeman and the boys get to know ya, why, you can stay down here for years!"

Thus began my life in the heady world of movies and television. Truth be told, once the shock wore off, I had a really good time in the old Print Department. Though Freeman turned out to be the equivalent of Frank Burns, "the boys" were a wacky, talented collection of Hawkeyes, Trappers and BJ's with aspirations similar to mine. Al was an extremely accomplished guitarist and Chuck, after several auditions, was about to be cast as the lead in a film based on the notorious Boston strangler. Tony Curtis apparently used some fancy choke holds of his own, because the producers eventually coughed up the part to "Tony-The-Star" rather than taking a chance on "Chuck-the-unknown." Chuck took the disappointment real hard and disappeared from the studio shortly thereafter—another unsung casualty of "Show-Biz!"

Sanctuary!

Eight hours of running a printing device known as a multilith machine was not exactly stimulating work. The constant, rhythmic sound of a spinning motor, blended with the fragrance from ink and toxic drum cleaner, dictated that the operator take as many breaks as possible. Our little gang took ours in a nice little courtyard adjoining the print shop. We munched away on items off the "roach-coach" (lunch wagon) and engaged in playful banter with a constant stream of secretaries (as assistants were known then) making their daily trips to collect freshly-printed script pages. Knowing the monotony ahead of us, we crammed jokes, crazy stunts, and as much laughing into twenty minutes as humanly possible. If the studio lot were a zoo, we were the gibbon cage.

In an attempt to compete with a fledgling public-tour program offered by rival studio, Universal, Fox decided to open its gates to a Hollywood touring company and offer trips around the lot in big, comfortable buses rather than the dreary little trams Universal used. Every day, six of these sleek, giant beauties would prowl the lot, stopping at various points of interest to allow for snap-shots and general gaping.

Well, pardners, it just so happened that in order to get to the "western street," the tour bus had to pass directly in front of the little print shop courtyard—and its schedule just happened to coincide with our breaks.

It didn't take long before I realized that we had a captive audience out there. We'd all but exhausted our secretary routines and were ready for some new form of amusement.

One day, at the sound of an approaching tour bus, a stirring scene from an old movie flashed into my head. I impulsively reached under our patio table and grabbed the thick, rusty chain anchored to an iron post embedded in the concrete. As the bus grew nearer, I wrapped the chain around my ankle, scrunched my hair straight up, and sat staring into space. My printing buddies looked at me, figuring that either the ink fumes had finally pushed me over the edge, or a new prank was about to be hatched!

Transforming myself into a hunch-backed Charles Laughton begging for water, I dropped my head, threw my shoulders forward, twisted my face and staggered wildly toward the oncoming bus shouting, "Wwatuhh, wwatuhh!" The chain even cooperated perfectly by snapping tight and jerking me to a halt within two feet of the bus, thereby saving the passengers—and myself—from a horrible fate. Frenzied tourists began snapping pictures of me like paparazzi at a studio premiere. From under his official bus-captain's hat, the apoplectic driver just glared at me.

Watching the bus pull out of sight, I'll never forget the great pride I felt as I turned to see all my cohorts in various stages of hysterical laughter. In fact, I think we all laughed until the next day when a small crowd gathered to watch me repeat the performance. Again the driver glared, the cameras flashed, and we laughed 'til our stomachs hurt.

Apparently, my antics were more appreciated than I realized. One memorable day, the driver stopped the bus, got out and made a bee-line right for me. To my utter astonishment, he explained that two more busses had been scheduled for the tour—could I appear for them too?

I promised to check with my agent.

No, it didn't lead to stardom. A couple of weeks later, the tour business was abruptly eliminated. I can say proudly, however, that I was the first and last stunt show ever offered by 20th Century Fox. And my courtyard performance did earn me a new nickname: IGOR. Apparently, my characterization was inaccurate, or none of my friends had ever seen Charles Laughton in *The Hunchback of Notre Dame.*

But opportunity was to strike again. The studio's Executive building had its own mail carrier and Xerox operator who serviced its elite tenants and I was offered the position of the "Xerox Guy," instantly trading dirty clothes and sticky ink for Xerox toner, slacks, and a tie.

Larry was my mail counterpart. Together, we shared an office on the first floor and controlled the flow of mail and inter-office memos between all producers and executives, including President Richard Zanuck. Larry made several major runs per day, picking up all the office mail, sorting it, and supervising its proper collection by the studio's main mail department.

My job was to wait for a secretary to call me, race two or three flights up to her office for the order, then race back down to my office, Xerox the material, and race right back up to her—ASAP! Multiply this activity by the approximately two hundred secretaries in the building, and you can understand how I managed to stay very fit.

Larry and I kept the building humming and had a lot of fun doing it. A very sexy, scantily-clad actress (let's call her Edwina) never failed to stop by our office on the way to her weekly roof-top liaison with one of the older in-house producers. Showing no mercy, she enjoyed taunting us by proudly displaying her latest tattoo or especially-toned body part. As soon as she heard the sound of our tongues hitting the linoleum, she would sashay on down the hall and through a little door leading to a stairway up to a secluded section of the roof. Moments later, the producer would emerge from his office, make sure the coast was clear, and nonchalantly disappear through the same door. Our chests swelled with dutiful pride knowing that we had "warmed up" Edwina for the benefit of one of our esteemed colleagues.

Then there was the mail boy (now a famous director) who delighted in staging fainting spells directly in the path of executives returning to their offices from lunch. Gasping for air, he would collapse at their feet, showering the startled execs in a flurry of letters. A funny scene I will never forget.

During my "Xerox guy" days, I made the acquaintance of a studio casting director who was also a talented, aspiring singer. Before long, we became fast friends. When a position as an assistant casting director became available, he was responsible for helping me get the job. In the blink of an eye, I got to drive my car onto the lot, wear neat suits, and meet a lot of friendly actresses.

Comedy Tonight

Attending school as an overweight kid presents you with three options: Take karate lessons so you can beat up all your tormentors; lose those extra pounds; or completely disarm the playground bullies by making them laugh. I chose the latter strategy.

In high school, I learned that my basic defense mechanism had a semi-respectable name—acting. Be it a play, talent show, or bake sale, I pursued every opportunity to perform that Alhambra High had to offer. Hearing audiences laugh filled me with a sense of well-being that would make even the most blissful guru envious. I was hopelessly hooked. Any plans my parents had for my discovering the cure for anything were washed away by the delicious sound of applause.

Another guy always showed up to audition for every part I wanted. Our short-lived rivalry evolved into a friendship as we discovered that we were *both* pretty funny. At least we thought so. To find out if anybody else did, we wrote a little act and offered our comedic services to parties and Moose Lodge charity events. We were such a hit that Moose signed us to an exclusive deal, thus effectively pre-empting the Elks.

Garrett & Maxwell, as we billed ourselves, began to gain some notoriety in our hometown and, with the help of Lori, our friend and "manager," we often pulled masters of ceremonies gigs at city functions. One in particular featured a local band led by another ambitious, young Alhambran named Kenny Loggins. It's important to note here that Kenny hired us to write special comedy material for his band and still owes us fifty bucks for it. Kenny, if you read this, please contact my publisher to arrange for payment. Installments are okay if you need a little more time.

Garrett & Maxwell developed into a fine little comedy team. By day I worked at Fox, with my nights reserved for performing in local nightclubs. We were hired by the USO to perform for the military fighting in Viet Nam. A few days prior to our departure, the war grew too intense for a couple of unarmed comedians and our eight-week performance tour was switched to Japan, Guam, Philippines...and Korea. Five years after this first trip, the USO once again hired us for another tour. It was then that I would visit a real MASH unit in Korea. Anyway, the studio wasn't all that anxious to give me a two-month vacation, so I had to make a career choice. Did I want to keep my coveted parking space, my cool position as assistant casting director, and, eventually become a movie studio executive? Or, in the grand tradition of Bob Hope, did I want to entertain our troops overseas and get paid to see the world?

I jumped on the plane.

A few years later, I was back at Fox visiting my casting director friend. He suggested that I take a break from clubs and might enjoy working as an extra on some episodic television shows. A little travel weary, I gave him the green light and he immediately plugged me into a show rumored to be in jeopardy of cancellation. I was told to report to a desolate section in the hills of Malibu, forty miles from my house, at five o'clock in the morning—not a great hour for a guy working in nightclubs until 2 A.M.

When I arrived on the set—a large clearing in the mountains peppered with funky old Army tents—I was greeted by an older fellow with a clipboard and a bad attitude. He gave me a quick once over and ordered me to get into my fatigues and then into make-up for a haircut. A haircut? Oh no, thank you. For a terrifying moment, I felt like I really *had* been drafted.

Outfitted in Army green, cap pulled down over my ears to hide my hair, I stumbled around the compound looking for the secret underbelly of production. What I found was a scene of almost overwhelming chaos: A hundred or so people yelling and screaming, running in all directions moving lights, cameras, jeeps, trucks, clothes, and small farm animals. I got through the gig all right, but I positively hated everything about the day, and vowed never to come back.

Exhausted, I returned home to find a disturbing message waiting for me. Because a scene I appeared in had to be shot from a different angle, my presence was required to "match" the action. Lucky me, I got hired again to report at five o'clock, "rain or shine," for another day of punishment at the good ol' Fox ranch.

Now, more familiar with the territory, I had no hesitation about clowning around with the actors, extras, crew, and even a few of the farm animals. At the end of the day I felt a suprising camaraderie, a sense of belonging—as well as some nasty blisters from my combat boots.

I soon attracted the attention of the first assistant director, Len Smith, Jr., who evidently was a connoisseur of world-class mugging. Len "cast" me in the non-speaking part of a soldier taking grief from Frank Burns (Larry Linville) who wanted some rocks on the compound newly painted. As he supervised my work, Colonel Blake (McLean Stevenson) advised Burns that the brighter rocks would provide too much of a target for enemy aircraft. Looking at me, Burns barked,"Then turn 'em over at night, private!" My "job" was to watch Burns walk away like he was crazy. The camera stayed on my face for what seemed like a half hour. Several "you're crazy" faces later, I heard laughter from Gene Reynolds, the director, and then from the entire crew. Gene finally yelled "cut!" and I let out a satisfied sigh of relief.

The comedy team of Garrett & Maxwell

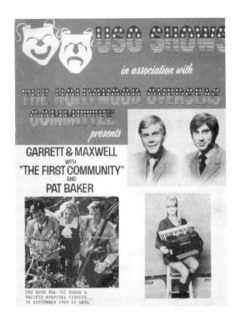

Posters for the two Garrett & Maxwell USO tours. We took the lovely Pat Baker with us on both tours—we were funny, not stupid.

The next day, I received congratulations from just about everybody for my very funny turn. Riding high, I went right into hunchy old Chuck Laughton for several cast and crew members. Like my print shop cohorts, they had never seen that Notre Dame flick either. From that day on, my official nickname on the M*A*S*H set was Igor.

Six Words to Stardom

It is traditional on some shows to give the extras, or "background artists," opportunities for speaking roles called "under fives." These hotly-pursued plums go to characters in a scene who are required to speak five lines of dialogue or less. To their credit, the M*A*S*H assistant directors were quite fair about circulating these high-paying upgrades-to-actor among the regular extra crew known as the mini-M*A*S*H cast, so like every other hopeful, I hunkered down and waited patiently.

I came to the acting business from the rough and tumble world of nightclubs. Wild audiences had poured beer on my head; a guy in Elko, Nevada, once tried to strangle me for lampooning General Patton, and during our Asia-Pacific USO Tour, the entire troupe of The Garrett & Maxwell show had been almost shot dead by trigger-happy Korean guards protecting the American Army base. So nothing or nobody in the performance arena, including consummate actors like Alan Alda, could intimidate me. Until, that is, the day I finally got to be an "under-fiver."

The first words I ever spoke on national television were directed to Radar, played by Gary Burghoff. In this particular episode, Radar had supposedly fathered a baby with a Korean girl and I was to play the role of a soldier in the chow line next to him. The part called for me to nudge him teasingly and say, "You son-of-a-gun, you." Since the scene was the first one up tomorrow, I diligently practiced my six words the night before and felt ready.

The next morning, I showed up on the set bright and early, with my line exceedingly well prepared. Not a butterfly within a hundred miles of my stomach until I saw the director—none other than the legendary former child star, Jackie Cooper. I was suddenly weak in my knees. With little warning, he yelled "action!" and I struggled to say something about seeing a baby with a gun.

After the first take, I turned toward Mr. Cooper, for directorial guidance, but no such luck. He looked at me like something had just gone wrong with his underwear, grunted a thank you to Gary, and trundled off for a donut. For better or worse, my network television acting debut was in the can.

Photo by Neal Gechtman

Garrett & Maxwell all fired up.
photo by Neal Gechtman

Just Stand There

One episode of *M*A*S*H* took four days to complete. The first was a rehearsal day for the cast and a few key members of the camera and lighting crews. The second, third, and fourth were long, ten-hour shooting days. Because a one-camera television show is shot in sections, actors are required to be on the set only if their character is in a scene scheduled to be filmed. If not, they are free to: go home, stick around and suck up to the producers, or generate an appearance in a tabloid by shamelessly making out in a trendy restaurant with a disheveled partner of the opposite, same, or newly-minted sex.

In the early days, my services as a regular extra were only required a couple of days a week. One day would always be on location at the Fox (as in 20th Century) Ranch for exterior shots and the other back at the studio for interiors.

One afternoon, the assistant director took me aside to gauge my interest in becoming a more permanent part of the family. He indicated that Alan Alda's stand-in wasn't working out and needed to be replaced immediately. The other stand-ins had been consulted and my name came up as an acceptable choice for the position. Because of Alan's enormous role on the show, I could expect to work ten hours a day, four days a week...and sometimes five.

Imagine, the staff choosing me to take over for Alan in the event he came down with the flu or just decided to go skiing in Switzerland for a few weeks! I was duly flattered and accepted the offer at once.

But I soon discovered that the occupation of stand-in had nothing to do with the theatrical position known as "stand-by" or "understudy." My sole duty was to substitute my body for Alan's while the lights were adjusted and camera moves rehearsed. Okay, I was a little disappointed about never assuming the role of Hawkeye, but I did enjoy steady employment, and just standing there allowed me to feel very confident in front of a motion picture camera.

Lighting, camera, and sound crews depend on the stand-ins to accurately recreate the actors' moves. This allows all the technical issues to be resolved before the expensive stars are brought back to shoot the scene. It was important, therefore, for me to watch Alan carefully during rehearsal so that I could reproduce his actions for the crew. In the course of doing my job, I developed a true appreciation for Alan Alda's impressive stamina.

For nine of the eleven years of production, I watched him work five days a week from seven A.M. to seven P.M., tirelessly breathing real life into the character of Hawkeye. Remember, this guy was not only acting every day, he also wrote and directed many episodes. And he commuted back and forth to New Jersey to be with his family on the weekends. His elegant command of the craft; his ability to sustain a constant level of focused energy and sense of humor, not to mention his genius for making everything seem so easy, was, in a word, astounding.

I could be darned funny in night clubs, but Alan inspired me to learn more, much more, about the nuts and bolts of acting. I really wanted to know how to do what he was doing. On his recommendation, I studied with a woman (now deceased) named Viola Spolin, the mother of improvisational theater. Later, another fine teacher, Stephen Book, took over her classes attended by then up-and-coming folks like Robin Williams and a host of others.

Up to that point, all of my dramatic training had been with the Royal Academy of Trial & Error. The more I learned about acting, the more I recognized and appreciated the talents of every single member of the gifted *M*A*S*H* ensemble.

Not too long after being drafted as a permanent member of the troupe, I was alerted to a part for me in an upcoming episode. I eagerly thumbed through the script looking for the part of "Soldier 1" or "Soldier 2" and found nothing. Disappointed, I expressed my confusion to the assistant director, Len Smith, Jr. He smiled and suggested I look more carefully. On my second pass. I found a scene in the mess tent that included the character of a server who was bantering with Hawkeye and Trapper about the lousy food. I read the scene three times before the light bulb came on. *M*A*S*H* writers often integrated real life experiences of the cast into a number of episodes. To my surprise and delight, the befuddled server behind the steam table had a name—Igor.

Where's The Party?

The allure of swinging Hollywood with its wild parties and Pagan-esque lifestyles has been around since the first celluloid frame rolled through a studio camera. Who among us hasn't been titillated by legendary stories of scandalous unions between popular actors and bikini-clad starlets, eager for a hunk of fame, a famous hunk, or just a hunk o' fun weekend.

Okay, I'll admit it. In my earlier years, the prospect of sipping bubbly amidst the giggles of an admirer or two offered some appeal. It was time for me to follow in the footsteps of my ribald, theatrical forebears and devour the luscious fruits of self-destruction.

So what happens? I do the impossible by landing a spot on a hit television show, and the actors, producers, and writers all turn out to be a bunch of grown-ups. Not a "Heather" among 'em!

Take, for instance, Gene Reynolds, the Executive Producer (boss), and Emmy award winning director of numerous *M*A*S*H* episodes, including the pilot. Never resorting to phony histrionics or ego trips, Gene's vast experience in motion pictures and television was all he ever needed to fully galvanize both cast and crew. You always knew when he was on the set—everyone seemed to move just a little quicker. I used to get the biggest kick out of watching him watching the scene being shot. His facial expressions would reflect every emotional moment being played by the actors. After a long day of directing, he must have gone home at night with a sore face. It was a true pleasure to see him guide our show from scene to scene with confidence and dignity. Gene served as the President of The Directors Guild of America for four years. They were lucky to have him.

Mozart could "hear" music in the ethers; Mohammed Ali could float like a butterfly and Larry Gelbart's remarkable brain can manipulate words faster than you can finish reading this sentence. One day, Larry was summoned from his office to help with a scene that wasn't playing so well. In a stunning display of his writing genius, he watched a run-through, instantly made notes on each of the actors' scripts, and then asked for the scene to be repeated with his hand-written changes. It played perfectly. Whether credited or not, Larry wrote most of the first four years of the show. At the end of his watch, I asked him why he had decided to leave. He gazed thoughtfully for a moment across the brightly lit set of the 4077th and said, "I'm just tired."

Burt Metcalfe worked on *M*A*S*H* as a casting director, associate producer, director, producer, and finally, executive producer. I wonder if he ever ran a printing press.

Anyway, this man grew into a talent that filled some pretty formidable shoes. He learned from the best and eventually assumed the reins of a runaway hit, driving it across the finish line with graceful aplomb.

All three of these men left their own personal stamp on the show. One can argue the merits of changes in cast, character attitudes and story direction. What cannot be debated is the remarkable (still unmatched) ratings record set by the final 2½-hour special, "Goodbye, Farewell and Amen." *Everybody* must have done something right. And that included a host of talented writers, along with accomplished directors like Jackie Cooper, Hy Averback, and Charles Dubin.

And, of course, there was Alan Alda—a man with a wildly playful, creative sense of humor emanating from a deeply serious and committed soul. Labeled "sensitive" by the press, Alan exhibited the kind of toughness that only befits someone willing to acknowledge and explore his own complicated humanity.

Wayne Rogers, very much like his "Trapper" character, had a refreshingly comfortable sense of ease about him. Along with his *M*A*S*H* duties, he was also seriously involved in the world of business and finance. After he finished a shot he'd usually head right for the phone to wheel and deal. I always hoped to make enough money to invest big in one of his projects—I'm still hoping.

Mike Farrell succeeded at a tough assignment—replacing a popular predecessor on a mega hit show. His thoughtful determination and tenacity helped "B.J." evolve from the "new guy" into a forceful and important character.

*I visited the 43rd Surgical Hospital while on tour in Korea, 1974. Note the TV M*A*S*H poster behind me.*

Loretta Swit should be an inspiration to women—and men, too. She was surrounded by an all-male cast—with hardly a female writer or producer in sight. Her strength and talent allowed her to succeed and flourish where others might have faltered.

Larry Linville's portrayal of Frank Burns was outstanding. For years, he made a difficult, over-the-top character absolutely real and believable. Watching Larry sail through a scene that required complicated physical and emotional "moments" was a valuable lesson in concentration. Though at times troubled by romantic problems, his good-natured personality was a pleasure to be around.

Jamie Farr was sheer dynamite. His crafted, energetic portrayal of Klinger brought

This is the real thing in Korea—not a studio prop.

believability to a character that could easily have been perceived as ridiculous.

William Christopher turned being nice into an art form. His quiet sense of humor and genuine goodness made it easy for everyone to respect the "gentle Padre" in him.

McLean Stevenson, hands down, was the funniest person on the set. More than a few scenes were stopped cold by his sudden improvisational riffs that put everybody in stitches. He drove himself to achieve excellence in his performance and from the show. I once ran into him on an NBC audition when he was shooting "Hello, Larry," a series he did post *M*A*S*H*. After learning why I was there, he walked me right into the producer's office and "sold" me for fifteen minutes straight. I got the job, but the pilot tanked. McLean's sincerity and humor made him a beacon on stage 9, as well as in the hearts and minds of his fans. He was a great guy.

Harry Morgan deserves any and all awards show business has to offer. Any actor would kill to have Harry's command of the craft. A true role model, it knocked me out to be in a scene with him knowing that he had worked with the likes of Gary Cooper, Spencer Tracy, and Fredric March.

David Ogden Stiers is a very fine actor who continues to display his talent in a variety of roles. In stark but amusing contrast to the pompous Winchester character was David's daily arrival to the set on his skateboard.

Gary Burghoff is an advanced, spiritual being whose respect for and appreciation of life is rare, especially in show business. His grace and sensitivity allowed him to share the innocence in Radar that we all loved.

Then there were all the great behind-the-scenes people like Len Smith, Jr., David Hawks, Dominic Palmer, Marty Lowenheim, William Jurgensen, Doug Stubbs, Karen Lieberman, Carol Pershing, Scott McDonald, Will Yarbrough, and Stephen Bass, to name but a few. For eleven years, these folks—and many more—were known on the lot as "the happiest crew in Hollywood."

No, hardly a group you would find romping through tabloids or skinny-dipping at a Beverly Hills pool party. As TV shows go, this was about as classy as it gets. To be perfectly honest, I did miss "Heather"—just a little.

That's A Wrap

After a few years of pulling double duty, I resigned my commission as Alan's stand-in to pursue other show business opportunities as an actor, writer, and producer. Fortunately, the executive staff continued writing Igor into the show and allowed me to happily slop food onto the trays of all the characters of the 4077 right up to the very end.

Those mess tent scenes were usually the first to be filmed in the morning with all the food provided by the studio commissary. Our prop guys would mush it up so it would appear less than appetizing, but it actually was quite tasty. During rehearsals I eagerly wolfed down the very bacon, eggs, and toast that sat limply on that infamous steam table.

Some have said that the role of Igor was more like a biscuit. Ha ha. I'll admit it would've been nice if between seasons he had gone to medical school and become Dr. Igor. However, I want to state very clearly how lucky and grateful I am (except for the first couple of days) for every single moment of the nine unforgettable years I spent working on this once-in-a-lifetime experience known as *M*A*S*H*. I grew up with *the* best. Twenty-five years later, to all the members of the cast, crew, and production staff—a big "Thank you" and a very big "I miss you."

Early days on the 20th Century Fox "Hello Dolly" street.

To some of the executives of Twentieth Century Fox and those of you who might be considering a career in television—keep on bowling!

CALL SHEET — TWENTIETH CENTURY-FOX FILM CORPORATION

5TH DAY OF SHOOTING
SHOOTING CALL 8³⁰A
PICT. "M*A*S*H" — As TIME GOES BY — NO. 9-B10 — DIR. BURT METCALF
DATE FRI JAN 14, 19__

SET — EXT MOTOR POOL (N) 1,2,3,4,5,6,7 SCS. 21 — 3⅜ PGS. — STAGE C
 18,10
SET — PRESS CONFERENCE (1,2,3,4,5,6,7) SCS.

CAST AND DAY PLAYERS	PART OF	MAKEUP	SET CALL	REMARKS
1. ALAN ALDA	"HAWKEYE"	8A	8³⁰A	MAKEUP DEPT
2. MIKE FARRELL	"B.J."	8A	8³⁰A	
3. HARRY MORGAN	"POTTER"	8A	8³⁰A	
4. LORETTA SWIT	"HOT LIPS"	8A	8³⁰A	
5. DAVID OGDEN STIERS	"CHARLES"	8A	8³⁰A	
6. JAMIE FARR	"KLINGER"	8A	8³⁰A	
7. WILLIAM CHRISTOPHER	"MULCAHY"	8A	8³⁰A	
10 G W BAILEY	RIZZO	8A	8³⁰A	
16 KELLYE NAKAHARA (NEW)	KELLYE	8A	8³⁰A	

CLOSED SET
ABSOLUTELY NO VISITORS

- ALL CALLS SUBJECT TO CHANGE BY ASSISTANT DIRECTOR

ATMOSPHERE AND STANDINS — THRU GATE

5 STANDINS (GOLDMAN, HILL, BETTINGER, THOMPSON, TROY) — 8A — STAGE 9
3 GI'S (CLINE, DICKIE, SNIDER)
4 NURSES (DAVIS, FARRELL, JAY, SABA)

A D V A N C E

PRINCIPAL PHOTOGRAPHY COMPLETED
— END OF 11TH SEASON —

ASST. DIR. C. KINSOCK/B. GELMAN — UNIT PROD. MGR. D. HAWKS

*At the end of every day, a call sheet was handed to
each member of the cast and crew. It indicates all pertinent
information for the following day: actors' call times,
shooting schedules, etc. This is a copy of the final call sheet
which marked the end of production. Looking at it
still gives me the shivers.*

Jeff, the serious actor, listening intently to the director.

Jeff, the actor—

seriously blowing the scene.

• PHOTOS •

BY JEFF MAXWELL

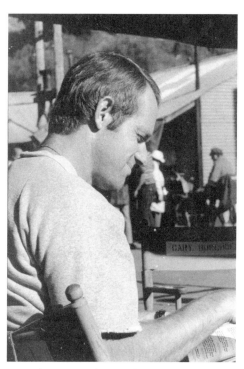

Gary Burghoff relaxes during a break.

A clean-cut Mike Farrell enjoys his script.

*Harry Morgan clowns with
George Simmons.*

*Jamie playing horse-shoes with
crew member, Vern.*

*"Careful Jamie, that's the boss
underneath you."*

*Roy Goldman and William Christopher
prepare to wheel "Donald Penobscot"
(Beeson Carroll) to his wedding ceremony.*

Gary Burghoff and crew watching a trainer try and convince his horse to lie down and play sick.

There was nothing fancy or glamorous at the Fox Ranch.

Roy explains to Private Igor why his mouth hangs open.

That's me looking for "direction" in my life.

All that hair was stuffed under "Igor's" hat.

Kellye "Nurse Kellye" Nakahara worries about snakes.

First Assistant Director, David Hawks, checks the script for our next shot.

Roy and Dennis, stand-ins with the show for 11 years.

Dennis practicing his "stunt."

Gwen Farrell, boom-man, Will Yarbrough, and Jennifer Davis test out a cot in the swamp.

Our propman, Doug Stubbs, was always lugging body parts.

Something distracts dialogue coach Marty Lowenheim, from his script.

Executive Producer, Gene Reynolds, hoping somebody will come through those doors.

Executive Producer, Burt Metcalfe, proves that it's lonely at the top.

This perennial game of Hearts lasted nine years.

Okay, it wasn't all work.

*The crew waits for somebody to put the camera
back on the camera boom.*

*Marty Lowenheim, Will Yarbrough,
Burt Metcalfe, and David Hawks
ready for "action."*

Jeeps and reflectors standing at attention.

• M*A*S*H FACTS •

* MASH stands for Mobil Army Surgical Hospital.

* *M*A*S*H* originated as a book written by Dr. Richard Hornberger. It was a fictional account of his Korean War experiences while stationed at the 8055 MASH. Dr. Hornberger wrote under the pseudonym of Richard Hooker.

* Made into a feature film in 1970 by 20th Century Fox, it featured Elliot Gould as Trapper John, Donald Sutherland as Hawkeye Pierce, Robert Duvall as Frank Burns, and Sally Kellerman as Hot Lips. The screenwriter, Ring Lardner, Jr., won the Academy Award for Best Screenplay.

* *M*A*S*H* premiered as a television series on CBS on September 17, 1972.

* Gary Burghoff was the only actor from the film to continue in his role of Radar for the run of the television series.

* The original series cast featured Alan Alda as Hawkeye, Wayne Rogers as Trapper John, Loretta Swit as Margaret "Hot Lips" Houlihan, Larry Linville as Major Frank Burns, Gary Burghoff as Radar, McLean Stevenson as Colonel Blake, William Christopher as Father Mulcahy, and Jamie Farr as Max Klinger. Later cast changes included Harry Morgan as Colonel Potter, Mike Farrell as B.J. Hunnicut, and David Ogden Stiers as Major Winchester.

* The show won a total of 44 awards: 14 Emmy Awards, 9 People's Choice Awards, 4 Directors' Guild Awards, 6 Writers' Guild Awards, 4 Golden Globes, 6 Eddie Awards (Editing), and The George Foster Peabody Award for broadcast excellence.

* *M*A*S*H* ran 11 years on CBS from September of 1972 until February 28, 1983.

* The episode "As Time Goes By" was the last show ever shot. It was produced after the 2½-hour special.

* "Goodbye, Farewell and Amen," the 2½-hour movie that concluded the series, set a television ratings record that remains unbroken and unmatched as of this writing. It was viewed by over 125 million people, more than half the population of the United States.

Now you know what it looked like behind the bar in the Officers Club.

• INDEX •

INDEX

INDEX

R

Radar's Teddy Bear Turkey Loaf, 86
R & R Hot Crab Dip, 203
Rapid Fire Fusilli, 164
Raspberry Sauce, 222
Rat-A-Tat Touille, 162
Red Alert Tortillas, 204
Reuben sandwich, 51
rice
  Dress White Rice, 150
  P'Anmunjombalaya, 82
Ricotta cheese, 168
River of Liver, 128
Rizzo's Motor Pool Penne, 166
Rosey's Red Chili Pork, 157
rum
  Colonel Flagg's Truth Serum, 227
  Nurse Sherie's Creamed Whiskey, 229
  Suicide Is Painless, 232
  UN Troop Toast, 29

S

salad dressings
  Anchovy Salad Dressing, 64
  Caesar Salad Dressing, 60
  Gorganzola Vinaigrette Dressing, 54
  Roquefort Sour Cream Dressing, 57
Salad, Off Base Korean, 156
salads, 52-65
  Winchester's Wilted Lettuce, 171
salami, 5
salmon
  Brigadier Broiled Salmon, 92
  Sidney Freedman's Nervous Breakdown
    Breakfast, 9
  Sparky's Sockeye Salmon and Vegetable
    Hash, 96
sandwiches, 40-51
sauces
  Balsamic-Pepper Sauce, 159
  barbecue, 110
  bruschetta, 76
  Cayenne-Lemon Butter, 193
  chili sauce, 74
  Dijon Ranch Sauce, 92
  Pasilla Chile Sauce, 102
  pork chop sauce, 108
  Raspberry Sauce, 222

Sweet and Sour Pineapple Sauce, 200
  Tomatillo Sauce, 120
  Tomato Sauce, 125
scallops
  Scalpel Scallops, 95
  Supply Clerk Scallops, 102
  Three-Day-Pass Pasta, 104
seafood, 92-107. See also lobster, scallops,
  shrimp, snapper, sole, swordfish, tuna
Section 8, 182-233
Sergeant Bustyer Gutt's Lasagna, 168
Shake, Pre-Op Novocaine, 231
Shell-Shocked Crab and Cheese Bread, 47
Sherman's Great Caesar's Salad!, 60
Shrapnel Salad, 63
shrimp
  Colonel's Kernel Stew, The, 70
  Company Clerk Quiche, 71
  Hawkeye Pierce's Pickled Shrimp, 192
  Incubator Shrimp, 193
  Movie Night Popcorn Shrimp, 200
  P'Anmunjombalaya, 82
  Pierce's Poached Eggs, 8
  Rizzo's Motor Pool Penne, 166
  Side-Arm Shell Salad, 64
  Spearchucker's Shrimp, 98
  Sweet and Sour Stretcher Shrimp, 205
  Three-Days-Pass Pasta, 104
Side-Arm Shell Salad, 64
Sidney Freedman's Nervous Breakdown
    Breakfast, 9
Slickee Boy Sweet Potatoes, 179
Snapper, Orange Sniper, 94
sole, 100
Sorry 'Bout That Father Creamed Corn, 39
soups
  Back-in-the-World Cabbage Soup, 67
  Cream of Weenie Soup, 32
  Creamy Veggie Soup, 36
Spaghetti, Hawkeye and Trapper's Swamp, 161
Spam Lamb, 131
Sparkey's Sockeye Salmon and Vegetable
    Hash, 96
Spearchucker's Shrimp, 98
spinach
  Creamed Green, 34
  Creamed Weenies, 72

INDEX

Photo by Richard Salvatore

Jeff Maxwell and his assistant, George.